MARCO

MAL LOR CA

SWITZERLAND

FRANCE

ITALY

Bilbao

ANDORRA

MC

Madrid

Barcelona

Corsica (F)

SPAIN

Mallorca

Valencia

Sardinia (I)

The Balearics

The Mediterranean

ALGERIA

fr.50

FREE!

THE TOURING APP

shows you the way...
including routes and offline maps!

GET MORE OUT OF YOUR MARCO POLO GUIDE

IT'S AS SIMPLE AS THIS

1 go.marco-polo.com/mlc

2 download and discover

GO!

WORKS OFFLINE!

SYMBOLS

INSIDER TIP Insider Tip

★ Highlight

●●●● Best of...

☼ Scenic view

♲ Responsible travel: for ecological or fair trade aspects

(*) Telephone numbers
that are not toll-free

**PRICE CATEGORIES
HOTELS**

Expensive over 130 euros

Moderate 80–130 euros

Budget under 80 euros

Prices per night for two people in a double room with
breakfast

**PRICE CATEGORIES
RESTAURANTS**

Expensive over 35 euros

Moderate 20–35 euros

Budget under 20 euros

Prices for a meal with starter,
main course and dessert, excluding drinks

CONTENTS

MAPS IN THE GUIDEBOOK
(146 A1) Page numbers and
coordinates refer to the road
atlas
(0) Site/address located off
the map
Coordinates are also given for
places that are not marked
on the road atlas
(U A1) Coordinates refer to
the map of Palma inside the
back cover

(🗺 A–B 2–3) refers to the
removable pull-out map
(🗺 a–b 2–3) refers to the in-
set map on the back of the
pull-out map

INSIDE FRONT COVER:
The best Highlights

INSIDE BACK COVER:
Map of Palma

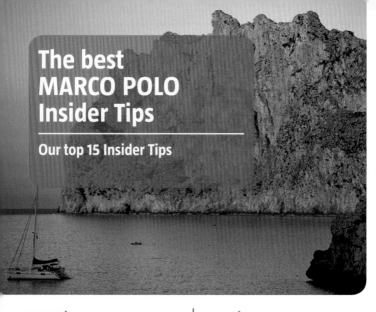

The best MARCO POLO Insider Tips

Our top 15 Insider Tips

INSIDER TIP **Shop beneath the stars**

Stay up late to browse the wares at a *fira nocturna,* or evening market. Handicrafts will whet your appetite for shopping, while you can satisfy any actual hunger pangs at a night-time food stand → p. 130

INSIDER TIP **Magic mountain**

The sun paints the *Cavall Bernat* mountain range in different colours – sometimes you even see a horse → p. 74

INSIDER TIP **Encounter of the third kind**

Travel 3,700 years back in time in 20 minutes on a beach walk from Can Picafort to *Son Real, City of the Dead* → p. 69

INSIDER TIP **Feast among the fishermen**

Take a seat amid the hustle and bustle in this small fishing harbour and enjoy the catch of the day: at the restaurant on the pier of *Cala Rajada* you have all the ingredients you need for a perfect fish dinner → p. 67

INSIDER TIP **Relax!**

You don't go to the *Son Caliú Hotel* for sleeping – non-residents are welcome in the great spa area → p. 52

INSIDER TIP **Alternative Palma**

For themed walking tours with itineraries taking in the Jewish quarter, Art Deco architecture, monasteries, commercial centres or monumental buildings, try *Mallorca Rutes*. Tours are available in several languages, and the guides really know their stuff → p. 32

INSIDER TIP **Underwater elevator**

At the *Cabrera Visitor Centre* you can immerse yourself in the sub-aquatic world of the national park with the help of a panoramic lift that takes you down into the subterranean aquarium landscape → p. 95

INSIDER TIP **Eat global**

In Palma's trendy district of *Santa Catalina* you can taste food from around the world at over 80 international restaurants and bars → p. 37

INSIDER TIP Sweet and sticky

Beekeeper Marta tends to her bees as if they were her own children, and they reward her richly in return. Her delicious *Mel de na Marta* honey is sold at markets in Pollença, Sineu (photo below) and Artà → p. 30

INSIDER TIP Adrenaline-free adventures

Put on your wetsuit, switch on your torch, and head off into the *Cova des Coloms* – the cave of pigeons. It might sound adventurous, but it's perfectly safe – and totally spectacular, as the walls of the enormous caverns are reflected in the crystal-clear freshwater lake → p. 83

INSIDER TIP From basket to plate

Why cook for yourself when you have the *Cervecería Anfos?* Trini and Manolo buy their produce from the Mercat de l'Olivar and throw it straight into the pan on the spot. You can't get any fresher than that! → p. 37

INSIDER TIP Epicurean merienda

A sumptuous *pa-amb-oli* plate in a new oil mill might just be a snack for the locals, but it makes a good lunch for visitors → p. 101

INSIDER TIP Off the tracks

Art, tapas, cooking courses and dance lessons at the *Vi-és:* Creative Mallorcan gallery owners show you what's inside an old railway station → p. 105

INSIDER TIP Odds and ends for every occasion

Here you can find everything you never thought you'd need. *Can Garanya 40* is a glorious bric-à-brac store packed with day-to-day objects from Mallorca → p. 82

INSIDER TIP Chill out behind the scenes

The new restaurant *S'Oratge* in the coastal town of Sa Rapita may not overlook the sea, but the views would only distract you from the stylish-yet-relaxed atmosphere and the tasty food → p. 89

BEST OF...

FOR FREE

● Art & prayer
If you want avoid paying admission to see the *La Seu Cathedral* in Palma, attend a mass instead. Make sure to arrive ahead of time and grab a seat up front on the right. From this vantage point, you can enjoy Gaudí's swinging chandeliers and Barceló's ceramic masterpieces for the whole service → p. 42

● Off into the wilds
Fed up with all the crowds? Then do as the animals do, and go where the island is still wild. *S'Albufera* nature park is home to many protected species, and you can go for a wander through the wetlands here – which are free of asphalt, free of concrete, and free of charge (photo) → p. 71

● The entire Tramuntana in a single exhibition
You need to experience the magic of the Tramuntana mountains for yourself – but you can find out what makes this Unesco-protected cultural landscape so special at the info centre on the *Raixa* estate → p. 56

● A palace for everyone
Come in! Other than most palaces in Palma, the *Casal Solleric* opens its doors for visitors. Inside: a picture-perfect courtyard, an art exhibition and a library → p. 36

● The best organ in Spain
An organist blows air through 25 pipes at the push of a key – so imagine how it must sound when it's played properly! You can pay a lot of money for concert tickets to find out; or you can attend a free practice session at the church of *Sant Andreu* in Santanyí → p. 93

● At home with Joan Miró
Of course, it's well worth paying the 7.50 euro admission fee for the fantastic museum of the *Fundació Pilar i Joan Miró,* which is housed in the artist's former home – however, on Saturday afternoons and certain other days you can also get in for free → p. 35

(I I I) Dots in guidebook refer to "Best of..." tips

● *Red earth and white blossom*
Millions of magnificent pink-and-white blossoms on Mallorca's characteristic red soil: experience a unique natural spectacle during the almond blossom season from late January to early March, near Son Servera for instance, where it is even celebrated with a festival → p. 130

● *Bread with things*
This is the literal translation of the Mallorcans' *pa amb oli*. Integral parts of this delicious sandwich, apart from olive oil, are tomatoes, air-dried ham or/and island cheese, marinated sea fennel and capers: very good at the *Hostal d'Algaida* → p. 98

● *That bit closer to God...*
Every village has its *ermita*, *monasteri* or *santuari*, mostly atop the summit of a mountain, some of them converted into lodgings with picnic spots. For the islanders, those are sacred spots. Extended families meet for a barbecue, and hikers enjoy the views of their home island, e.g. near the *Ermita de la Trinitat* → p. 59

● *Sweet temptation*
Not even on the neighbouring islands will you find an *ensaïmada*, the coiled yeasty bun made with lard and sprinkled with icing sugar, as tasty and tender as on Mallorca. For proof, head for the *Ca na Juanita* bakery in Alaró, which has been going for over 100 years (photo) → p. 100

● *Cold pressed*
The label *Oli de Mallorca* can only be used for the olive oils native to the island. Mallorcan oils have been exported with great success for centuries, but local fine foods shops, supermarkets and *oil mills* like that in Sóller stock all kinds of creations → p. 55

● *Get some fresh air*
Late in the evening, Mallorcans make themselves at home on the street: *prendre la fresca* is what they call putting their chairs outside their front doors to enjoy the cooler evening air and chat about the events of the day. Do as the natives do and take to the bustling village squares of *Bunyola* or *Esporles* on any summer evening from 10pm onwards → p. 56, 59

ONLY ON

BEST OF...

AND IF IT RAINS?
Activities to brighten your day

● *Life in the seven seas*
Ever cuddled with a ray? Basins where you can touch the fish, snorkelling opportunities and shark tanks: The *Palma Aquarium* is interactive and exciting → p. 127

● *Going down*
The island's charms are also hidden beneath the earth: in thousands of caves, of which five are accessible to the public. The *Coves de Campanet* are small but perfectly formed. The sometimes spaghetti-thin stalactites and stalagmites are impressive → p. 71

● *White heat*
Gordiola near Algaida is the oldest of the island's three glass-blowing establishments. Do as the Spanish royal family did, watch the workers and admire fragile beauty (photo) → p. 97

● *For the love of film*
Passionate cinephiles make great company on a rainy evening. The *Cine Ciutat* is run by film fans as a cooperative, and screens international movies in a range of original languages with subtitles → p. 40

● *A spiritual journey through churches and cloisters*
Did you know that San Francisco was founded by a Mallorcan missionary? The building he was born in stands in Petra and forms part of the *Spiritual Mallorca* tour that takes you to the religious heart of the island with the help of an affordable package ticket – from the awe-inspiring cathedral in Palma to the heavenly heights of the Cura monastery → p. 100

● *Not just for Christmas*
In high summer this might seem bizarre to you, but the Neapolitan nativity scene in the *Palau March Museu* in Palma is worth a visit at any time of the year, filling an entire room of the palace → p. 36

RAIN

RELAX AND CHILL OUT
Take it easy and spoil yourself

● *Serenity in the spa*
Many hotels use the word "spa" to attract custom, but sometimes they just have a pool that is only open to guests. The spa in the *Lindner Golf & Wellness Resort* is open to the public and more than lives up to its name → **p. 45**

● *Relaxing stroll through the city*
Feet hurting from exploring Palma? Combine a visit to the *Banys Arabs* in the old town with a breather on one of the benches in the lovely gardens: take a deep breath in idyllic greenery and think back over what you've seen (see photo) → **p. 34**

● *Relax on the water*
Breathe in some sea air for an hour on a harbour cruise with *Cruceros Marco Polo*: there's nothing more comfortable than having Palma served to you from the sea → **p. 37**

● *Palma from high up*
You don't have to be a resident in the luxurious *Son Vida* castle hotel to order a coffee and enjoy the first-class service and unique views from the terrace → **p. 42**

● *Slow train to Sóller*
Trundle north from Palma on board the nostalgic *Ferrocarril de Sóller* and watch the lemon groves, tunnels and valleys as they roll past the window. The pleasant journey along this narrow-gauge railway lasts an hour – plenty of time to switch off and enjoy the scenery → **p. 54**

 ● *Sheer sunset*
When the sun goes down behind the Tramuntana mountain ranges and the lights of Port de Pollença begin to sparkle, high above at the foot of *Albercutx Tower* is the place to be. Enjoy this breathtaking moment as the crowning glory of a drive to the Formentor Peninsula → **p. 74**

CHILL OUT

11

INTRODUCTION

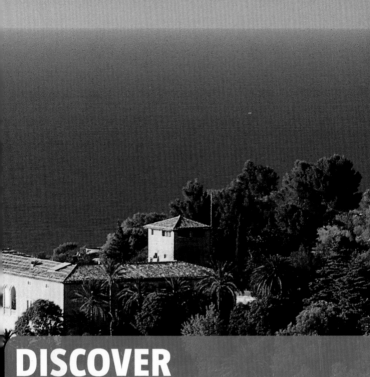

DISCOVER
MALLORCA!

Loud chatter of cicadas in your ear and the scent of pine in your nose, the sun burning down on you – and from below, shimmering through the green of the treetops, a turquoise bay with its white rim of sand: the Cala Mondragó is only one of hundreds of small sandy bays dotted all around the island. And of course this fits in perfectly with the dream image of *sun, sand and the Mediterranean*. That this area is also hardly built up and has been declared a strictly protected natural park shows ecological insight of a kind rarely encountered in the Mediterranean.

Mallorca is a magnet, and the largest island in the Balearics pulls them all in: kings, artists, pop stars, drop-outs and downsizers – and most of all tourists. No other Mediterranean destination is as varied and as versatile. Infamous as a holiday destination for the masses in the early years of tourism, the island has developed into a multicultural microcosm with excellent infrastructure and high-quality gastronomy, without ruining Mallorca's most important resource: its *overwhelming natural beauty*. Visitors wanting to experience this have to be prepared to leave the hotel, the swimming pool and the resort beach, and to strike out on their own: on foot, by bike or motorbike, by local bus, train or hire car. Mallorca's road network is exemplary, prices for hiring a car no more expensive than elsewhere, and distances from east to west or from north to south don't exceed 90 km (56 miles).

The *history of tourism* on Mallorca has been both stormy and eventful. For Mallorcans, tourism became the economic miracle with the state-run expansion programme ordered by General Franco in the 1960s, a massive construction boom along the coastlines of Spain – and Mallorca in particular. Farmers and fishermen turned into service personnel, receptionists, waiters, chefs, restaurateurs, hotel directors, bus drivers, travel agent staff and guides. Today, tourism and associated sectors of the economy account for about 80 per cent of gross national product.

Mallorca is currently undergoing an *image overhaul*, with a trend towards greater sustainability, higher-quality hotel and restaurant offerings and a longer season. Families, active holidaymakers, culture vultures and nature-lovers are always welcome – particularly during the low season– and the island is trying to get rid of the binge-drinking crowd and lose its reputation as a cheap party destination.

> **A compact island where all destinations are within a 56 mile range**

What visitors can see across 3640 km^2/ 1405 square miles is far more than fits into a two-week holiday: *in the north, the large double bay* of Pollença-Alcúdia clasped between the two fingers of the Formentor and Isla de la Victoria peninsulas, the S'Albufera wetlands and the beautifully restored historic towns of Pollença, Alcúdia and Artà. *In the east, the pretty hills* of the Serra de Llevant with countless small paths leading down to just as many fjord-like coves, beaches and ports pretty as a picture. The *hot and flat south*, with its dune beaches and pine groves left in their natural state and its salt lakes is reminiscent of the neighbouring island of Ibiza even further south. Last not least, the cherry on the island's cake: *the wild west* with the imposing high mountains of the *Serra de Tramuntana,* counting over 40 peaks over 1000m/3280 ft, fathomless gorges and sky-high steep rock faces, not forgetting one of the most exciting and stunning drives in Europe. Last not least the centre, *es Pla,* a high plain with still somewhat sleepy villages, the cereal basket and vegetable garden of the island. There is also of course the capital, Palma, *one of the most beautiful cities of the Mediterranean*, which succeeds in preserving the old whilst creating something new, and which keeps reinventing itself –

round 4000 BC:
The first cave dwellers live on Mallorca

123 BC:
Romans occupy Mallorca, founding Pollentia and Palma; the island's first heyday

From AD 455 onwards,
Vandal incursions end Roman domination

From 903 onwards,
Mallorca is conquered by Arabic Moors and flourishes for a second time

1229
On 31 December a victorious Jaume I, King of Aragon, enters the Medina Mayurka (Palma), later destroying anything Islamic

The most famous building on the island: La Seu Cathedral in Palma

with museum pieces from an island history spanning 3000 years and trendy operations such as yoga and spa centres, shops stocking the latest fashions or cocoa boutiques.

Most summer visitors only spend one day in the capital; they have come for the sun, sand and sea and they will stick to it. Over *150 sandy beaches* with a total length of some 50 km (31 miles) are available to meet this wish, particularly as the water around the Balearics is considered the cleanest in the Mediterranean. There is hardly a beach not flying the Blue Flag, and hardly any section of the coast with effluents trickling into the sea. In any case the island is a Mediterranean pioneer of active protection of the environment. With the massive pressure exerted by the GOB environmental protection organisation on the island government in the

> **The cleanest water in the Mediterranean**

1276
Jaume II proclaims the Balearics as the Kingdom of Mallorca; Mediterranean trade flourishes under his successors and Ramón Llull elevates Catalan to a literary language

Up to 1561
Attacks by Turkish pirates

1814
After the end of Spain's Peninsular War against France, Mallorca is given its own liberal constitution

1905
Foundation of the Mallorcan tourist office Fomento de Turismo

1980s following intense construction activity, the local population also started rethinking the issue. The trend now is away from further urban spread through more and more new hotels and other tourist infrastructure towards a more environmentally sound, *soft tourism*; away from an overbearing foreign influence from outsiders towards preserving indigenous cultural values.

These days, the GOB is no longer fighting alone, as more and more private and also public initiatives are promoting *sustainable development* for Mallorca. Over the past decades, estates already sold to private buyers and investors, including whole bays, beaches and islands, have been bought back by the island government, and particularly threatened habitats such as the S'Albufera wetlands or the Cala Mondragó were declared *protected areas*. Last but not least, any construction in the entire Serra de Tramuntana, which after all constitutes a third of the island, is subject to very strict limitations. In 2011, the Unesco added these mountains in the north of the island to its list of World Heritage sites. This now means that special care has to be taken to keep the vineyards, olive groves, almond orchards and citrus plantations in good shape. The fruits of these labours can be bought at weekly markets and in fine foods shops around the island, including some organic products.

Leaving aside skiing and sledging there is nothing that you can't do on Mallorca. There are over 40 marinas, and water sports enthusiasts will find a wealth of facilities for *sailing, windsurfing and diving*.

> **Much room for outdoor activities on the steep coastline**

Visitors who don't want to be their own captain can book a boat tour, from half an hour with a simple pedal-powered boat through comfortable sightseeing tours aboard a pleasure steamer to an entire week cruising around the island on a yacht. Outdoor activities on the coast are gaining in popularity. The steep West and North coast leave much room for *canyoning, coasteering and climbing.* Both cyclists in colourful shorts and bikers enthuse about all the bendy mountain roads, and hikers just can't get enough of the fascinating interplay of mountains and sea.

Over 6,000 restaurants, cafés and bars offer a *broad range of culinary treats* for all tastes and budgets. Gourmets can feast to their heart's content (and expensively) in

From 1960 onwards:
After the construction of the first airport of Palma, mass tourism starts under General Franco

1983
The Balearic Islands become one of the 17 autonomous regions of democratic Spain; Catalan culture experiences a renaissance

2012
Spain's economic crisis brings difficulties for the tourist industry on Mallorca

2016
The crisis is over: Mallorca welcomes over 11 million visitors during its second record-breaking season in a row. The *Ecotasa* green tax is introduced

The unspoilt nature on the Sa Foradada peninsula can only be reached on foot or by boat

half a dozen *top restaurants*, while in any coastal resort those on a tighter budget will find enough cafeterías serving good-value menus that change daily or a large variety of tapas. Some like to pop the bubbly in *cool beach clubs*, others stick to the Happy Hour at crowded resorts. What do the Mallorcans have to say about this? Not much. Sometimes they take a drive to watch the tourists. Over the centuries, Mallorca has experienced a lot of occupation and foreign influence, with the Romans, Vandals and Arabs, with the Byzantines, and with Spaniards from the mainland. Acceptance and integration were always more the way of the island dwellers than resistance, even less so hatred. The foreign element was taken on board and slowly turned into something belonging to the island. What some criticise as the phlegmatic Mallorcan mentality others will see as *tolerance*. And in fact the island dwellers display a characteristic friendly reserve; interference and indiscretion are frowned upon. For the visitor this creates a *friendly atmosphere*, with at the same time an agreeable kind of distance.

When you come to Mallorca, the main thing you should bring with you is time, as life here moves at a sedate pace. *Poc a poc,* or "little by little" is the motto of the island, and its inhabitants try to live by it even during the busy season. So even if

poc a poc: **all in good time, the Mallorcan way**

not all your food is served at the same time in a restaurant, or you find yourself having to wait for service while shopping, then don't be impatient; instead, try soaking up a little bit of this poc a poc yourself and making it the motto of your holiday. And don't forget to take some of it back home with you too!

WHAT'S HOT

1 Cool sandals

Aubarcas Straightforwardly made, unbeatably comfy and cheap, these leather sandals actually originate from Menorca; however, they now serve as an everyday marker of regional identity and are worn all over the Balearic Islands. The authentic article comes with a sole made from old car tyres, but high heels and glittery materials are also acceptable. The best places to buy them are *alpargaterías* such as *La Concepción (C/ de la Concepció 17)* and *Blanc Mari (C/ Sindicato 34)* in Palma or *Ben Calçat (C/ Luna 74)* in Sóller.

Colourful concrete 2

Streetart Graffiti artists love the island's eyesores and have decorated hotels, building shells and roadside concrete walls. Enormous murals can be found around Plaça de Quadrado and Plaça Gomila or in the Terreno quarter in Palma; in the town centre of Muro; or on the Hotel Mar y Paz, the sports centre and an apartment block on Avinguda Diagonal in Can Picafort. For a virtual tour visit *www.instagram.com/streetart_mallorca*. In Peguera, the authorities of Calvià even organise the street art competition *Betart (www.pluscalvia.com/betart)*.

3 Vernacular music

Fascinatingly incomprehensible The Mallorcan *glosa* is a bit like American bluegrass music. Without musical accompaniment apart from the scratching rhythm of a Ximbomba, the *glosadors* sing improvised verses in Mallorcan dialect. With ambiguity and double entendre plus a dose of political satire, these folk music rappers continually recreate their songs. You have to have lived on the island for generations to truly understand what's being sung. Perhaps this is the reason why the *gloses* are becoming so popular again among the Mallorcans...

Island of ale

Craft beer   Microbreweries are proliferating like yeast in a fermentation tank, and there are already a dozen on Mallorca. Many of them are based in beautiful villages and brew their beers with water from the Tramuntana mountains. And how do they taste? Why not try them for yourself! It's particularly worth going on a tasting tour in Palma, where pubs like *Lórien (C/ de les Caputxines 5)*, *Guirigall (C/ Brossa 14)* and *Atomic Garden (C/ de Borguny 2)* have a large selection. The brewery *Sa Nau (C/ Bartomeu Pasqual 8 | www.cerveza.nau.com)* in Santa Maria del Camí sets up a bar between its fermentation tanks every Sunday from 10am until 3pm, while at *Sullerica (Camí des Camp Llarg 20 | book by calling mobile tel. +34 629 669 912 | www.sullerica.com)* in Sóller, visitors can even take a tour of the brewery – naturally with a tasting included!

Party atmosphere

Afternoon clubbing   After-work drinks were yesterday; today, it's time for *tardeo*. Every Saturday, Palma's party crowd goes dancing, drinking and flirting in the clubs of the island capital – and during the afternoon, no less (or in Spanish, *la tarde*). The main *tardeo* hotspots are *Sala Luna (Plaça Vapor 20)* and *Kaelum Club (Av. de l'Argentina 3)*. The action kicks off at around 2:30pm, as people meet for drinks and tapas at *Santa Catalina market hall (Plaça de la Navegació | www.mercatdesantacatalina.com)* before hitting the clubs around two hours later to really let their hair down. Things then tend to wind down at around 9pm.

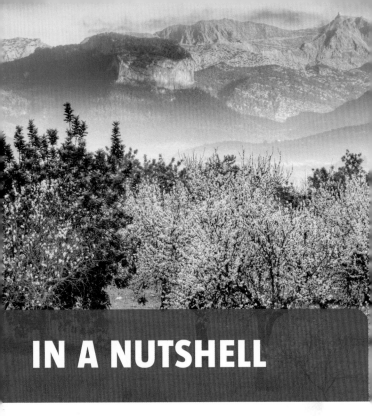

IN A NUTSHELL

BALEARIC ISLANDS

Most Mallorcans have never been to one of the neighbouring islands: Menorca, Ibiza or Formentera, which form the Balearic Archipelago. Together, these islands have nearly 1500 km/932 miles of coastline and 370 beaches; the regional capital city is Palma. The establishment of the autonomous community of the Balearic Islands in 1983 did little to create a sense of shared identity; interest among these island neighbours is growing, but slowly.

BON DIA

Mallorca belongs to Spain, of course, but the local language is (since the 13th century) *Mallorquí*, a Catalan dialect. During Franco's regime (1939–1975), *Mallorquí* was forbidden. That's why the locals love their language so much now. The politically correct greeting here is "bon dia" rather than "buenos días". Mallorcan Catalan is also the language of instruction and conversation at the local schools and universities. In Palma, where the majority of immigrants live, the main language you'll hear on the streets is Spanish, or *Castellano*. It can be a bit confusing – many town and road signs are written in two languages: the official Mallorcan (e.g. Peguera, Ses Salines) and the old Spanish (Paguera, Las Salinas). But don't worry too much about it – you're on vacation, so just relax!

CATALAN LUTHER

Tennis champion Rafael Nadal, Grand Prix motorcycle champion Jorge

Photo: Almond trees bloom before the peaks of the Serra de Tramuntana

Pirates are still talked about, and catapulting stones is a popular sport. But don't worry, everyday life on Mallorca is completely safe

Lorenzo and artist Miquel Barceló are the island's most famous native sons. But will people still remember them 700 years from now? When it comes to Ramon Llull (1232–1315/16), there's no question. The works of this lay theologist, philosopher and missionary are still taught at universities around the world. If you want to follow in his footsteps on his native island, explore the Randa hermitage, Miramar near Valldemossa or the Franciscan monastery in Palma (info: *www.rutasramonllull.com)*. Llull lived during the Crusades and the Reconquista, when Spain was retaken by the Christians. In the 13th century, the majority of Spain's population was Muslim. This vocal, non-conformist thinker preached dialogue rather than violence and made multiple trips to North Africa to debate Muslim philosophers in Arabic. Many of his writings were in Catalan rather than Latin; he is consequently considered the founder of the written Catalan language. In that sense, he's a bit like the Catalan Martin Luther.

CROWDED ISLAND

The locals aren't the only ones who think Mallorca is too crowded at peak times of year; many holidaymakers agree. The government is establishing growing numbers of nature reserves to offer a safe haven to both humans and the natural world. At the same time, the authorities on the island want to better distribute the flow of tourists. Palma will have reduced-traffic zones, and to avoid creating enormous crowds, visitors from cruise ships will no longer be carted to the La Seu Cathedral in their thousands; rather, they will be distributed more evenly across multiple tourist sights. The government is still debating a planned tourism law that would regulate the total number of hotel beds on the island.

ETERNAL SUMMER

Mallorcans are fed up with changing their clocks twice a year, and since they enjoy sitting outside on December evenings, the sun sets too early for them in the winter months. That's why the Balearic parliament unanimously (!) voted to apply to Madrid for permission to eliminate daylight saving time. At first, the politicians in Madrid just laughed. But then the regions of Valencia and Murcia joined the campaign. Will all of Spain soon do away with the central European time system?

FLYING STONES

For thousands of years, the indigenous people of Mallorca hunted animals and drove off intruders using *fones,* or slingshots. They were popular among the Roman legions for their accuracy. Today, Mallorcans are rediscovering the art of using these woven hemp slingshots in sport clubs; the best slingers can win awards in competitions. The projectiles are usually stones, but children often use tennis balls. Want to give it a try? You can see the masters compete at the traditional games expo in Biniali near Sencelles during the first weekend in June, and you can even give it a go yourself.

HOME TIES

Culturally, the residents of the island feel closest to Catalonia. Their language isn't the only obvious sign: FC Barcelona also has an enormous fan following on Mallorca. But many Mallorcans come from totally different regions of the country. There was a tourism and construction boom in Mallorca from the 1960s to the 1980s, and many of the island's current residents came from Andalusia or Galicia to work as builders, waiters or cleaners. Additionally, nearly 20 per cent of the island's approximately 860,000 residents come from outside of Spain – the majority are from Morocco, Germany (22,000) and Great Britain. There's little conflict between these diverse groups; the Mallorcans are far too relaxed for that. Many have come and gone, they say, referring to the island's long history of settlement and colonisation.

LIGHT & LIFE

Mallorca is green and bright throughout the year. The red earth, the white-pink almond blossom lasting from mid-January to March and the ripe oranges in winter dot all the green with colour. Some 1500 types of plant are known on the island. Summer visitors love the bougainvillea's red-and-purple riot of colour and oleanders lining entire streets. During the rainy winters, the underground cisterns fill up; live oaks, pines, almond, olive, carob, fig and lemon trees then draw water from them during the hot, dry summers. The millions of pink-and-white almond blossoms in January are the first harbingers of spring. They are followed in March by yellow and white marguerites that cover meadows and arable fields. April brings wild purple gladioli, May fire-red poppies. After the first rainfall of autumn, yellow sorrel and wild orange marigolds liven up the scenery. Evergreen oak forests cover 150 km²/58 square miles of the Serra de Tramuntana, and in the height of summer the extensive Aleppo pine forests resound with deafening cicada concerts.

The island may be rich in plant life, but there is no comparable abundance of animals. There are no larger mammals; what you will find are wild rabbits, field hares, martens, rats and mice, as well as feral goats whose teeth wreak a lot of damage. The island's fauna is dominated by birds. Some raptors in danger of extinction have been reintroduced. At the seaside, cormorants dive into the water; birdwatchers' hearts beat a lit-tle faster when they spot cinereous vultures or even Eleonora's falcons or puffinus on the virgin shores of Dragonera or Cabrera.

NOBLE ADMIRER

Long before the first onslaught of tourists, Habsburg Archduke Ludwig Salvator (1847–1915), known as *Arxiduc* in the Catalan language, fell in love with the island's beauty – and with a number of the local female beauties, as well. And while his many illegitimate descendants do not bear his name, several local roads and hiking trails are named after him. The islanders still honour him today, because he made their homeland internationally famous, particularly among the Viennese nobility. Even the famous Empress Sisi of Austria was mad about Mallorca. Salvator eventually retired to his Son Marroig estate above the Sa Forada-

Ramon Llull has developed a bit of a patina, but his works are still current: Memorial in Palma

Hiking in the Serra de Tramuntana nature reserve: a real contrast to the crowded island

da Peninsula near Deià. His book, "The Balearic Islands in Words and Images" remains an important source for historians and researchers of local traditions.

ORGANIC WINE

Mallorca's wines are getting better and better; the organic wines, in particular, regularly win awards. These days, one-third of wine-growers are using organic production methods. Spain's organic wine pioneer was Biel Majoral, which set up a little bodega *(www.canmajoral.com)* near Algaida in 1979. Ribas in Consell *(www.bodegaribas.com)*, Oliver Moragues in Algaida *(www.olivermoragues.com)*, Jaume Mesquida in Porreres *(www.jaumemesquida.com)* and Jaume de Puntiró in Santa Maria del Camí *(www.vinsjaumedepuntiro.com)* also produce sustainable wines. Many wine-growers are now planting native varieties of grapes once again, such as Manto Negro, Callet, Fogoneu and Gorgollassa, and pressing them in combination with Syrah, Cabernet or Merlot to create typical island wines. Further information: *www.bodegasmallorca.com*.

PARTY PEOPLE

...can mainly be found on Balneario 5 and 6, two sections of the long Platja de Palma beach. In the summertime, young party people from Germany stroll the "ham road" (Carrer Padre Bartolomé Salvá) and the "beer road" (Carrer Miquel Pellisa) amongst roving merchants, thimble-riggers and police. Priority number one for visitors to large bars like "Bierkönig" and "Bamboleo" is getting drunk, but there are many smaller pubs and restaurants in the area that cater to every taste. In the off-season, you'll also find families and groups of friends visiting the area for a quiet beach holiday. A number of bar and restaurant owners have banded together to launch a quality initiative called "Palma Beach"; they want to raise the standards in the area and attract new clientele, using Miami Beach as a model. An example of this initiative is the new design of the once-legendary beach kiosk Balneario 6, the original spot for beach-front binge-drinking. The bar was renamed *Beach Club Six* in 2017, and a small beer now costs 3.45 euros. Welcome to Miami!

PIRATES ON THE HORIZON?

There's an expression on the island: *Ara que no hi ha pirates.* Translated literally, it means, "Now, since there are no pirates here," meaning, "Now, since no one's looking." There's a difficult history behind this expression, and the the Mallorcans had to live with for centuries: pirate raids. The largest island in the western Mediterranean long served as an important port of trade, and Palma was home to wealthy merchants. But port cities like Pollença and Sóller also suffered raids by the Barbary Corsairs, who primarily came from North Africa. Even today, the *Moros y Cristianos* festivities in these cities serve as a reminder of this history; victorious battles against the invading forces are re-enacted. The watchtowers that line Mallorca's coast also tell a story of constant fear. Some even say that the rather tight-lipped nature of the island's residents is a result of this permanent threat; for their ancestors, the sea and the outside world were synonymous with danger.

SMUGGLER'S PATHS

Many of the hiking trails through the mountains and along the sea are paths once used by smugglers well into the 20th century to transport sacks of cigarettes, alcohol and coffee to their hideaways. These precious goods were then hawked by the ringleaders at a great profit. Speed boats were used to bring them to the island. The greatest modern-day smuggler was Joan March who was born in 1880 to a family of swineherds – later he was the richest man in Spain. Mallorca has his unscrupulous business sense to thank for its biggest and most beautiful fincas. March needed to unload his goods undetected, so he simply purchased large swathes of the coast. On S'Amador beach near Santanyí, a short, hidden path *(Itinerari de la punta de ses Gatoves)* leads through the seaside shrubbery. If you see a spacious hole in the wall on the site of the road, you've found a secret (hiding spot). Goods from Barcelona were unloaded on the east coast near Artà, in places like Cala Estreta. From there, a path leads to *Albarca Tower;* it takes about 75 minutes. It was constructed by the coast guard and, naturally, offers an excellent view of the sea. In the Tramuntana Mountains, take a 6-hour hike on the *Albarca, Cosconar, Puig Roig* Route through the smugglers' region, with beautiful views of the area around the Puig Roig mountain mass. In this spectacular rocky landscape, you'll also find the first border police checkpoint, now disused and in disrepair.

TALAIOTS

Talaia stands for watchtower or lookout tower. The derivation *talaiot* refers to prehistoric megalithic structures found on Mallorca and other Balearic islands. It is thought that those settlements, in existence from 1300 BC up to the Roman occupation, served religious purposes. In most cases, the watchtower, up to 8 m/26 ft high and erected from extremely heavy blocks of stone, would have stood at the centre of the settlement. Mallorca can boast over 100 such prehistoric settlements.

FOOD & DRINK

In spite of appearances, Mallorca's cuisine is not identical to Spanish cuisine. Certainly, paella and gazpacho, Rioja wines and sangria have long since conquered the islanders' palates, and olive oil is of course a great staple of Balearic cuisine.

While the majority of hotel kitchens, *cafeterías* and restaurants offer more international dishes than traditional regional ones, a separate *cuina mallorquina* does exist; it has however always been exposed to foreign influences, and still is. In the past this was owed to the Roman and Arab presence, today northern Europeans are contributing to changing recipes and eating habits.

One thing is certain: the island's cuisine cannot be reduced to "simple" or "hearty" fare, as is often said. The cooks of 18th-century feudal lords in particular created capricious, *delicate little dishes*; their recipes are now being rediscovered and cooked by enthusiastic restaurateurs. The only problem is however that even the more rustic cuisine of farmers and fishermen is fairly labour-intensive.

Mallorcan cooking means using *fresh produce* and taking particular care in its preparation. This type of cuisine doesn't like being chivvied along, least of all using ingredients from tins or the deep freezer. This means of course that the 1000-bed hotel with all-inclusive deals where meals are eaten in shifts in huge dining rooms cannot remotely do justice to the island's cuisine. You

Mallorcan cuisine combines several culinary styles – and even "simple" dishes need elaborate preparation

can get a simple and typical meal in one of the *Cellers*, rustic (cellar) restaurants, most with a wine bodega and pleasantly cool in the summer. Recommended authentic cellers: include *Can Ripoll* (see p. 99) in Inca, *Celler La Parra* (see p. 73) in Port de Pollença and *Es Celler de Manacor (www.facebook. com/EsCellerManacor)* where you sit amongst Majorcans.

In places where VIPs, the smart set and status-conscious *nouveaux riches* settle, *renowned chefs* are not far be-

hind. A handful of famous names stand for *international haute cuisine*, for example Josef Sauerschell with his restaurant *Es Racó d'es Teix, see p. 50)* or Marc Fosh *(Simply Fosh, see p. 39)*. Young island chefs like Marta Roselló, who cooks at *Sal de Cocó* (see p. 94) in Colònia de Sant Jordi, Andreu Genestra *(Capdepera | www.andreugenestra.com)* or Macarena Castro *(Restaurante Jardín | Port d'Alcúdia | www.res taurantejardin.com)* enrich the culinary landscape with *traditional knowledge*

LOCAL SPECIALITIES

albergínies farcides – aubergines filled with mincemeat

allioli – garlic mayonnaise served with meat dishes

arròs brut – "dirty rice" named thus for its saffron colouring; rice stew with three types of meat (photo right)

coca – Mallorcan version of pizza with a yeasty dough topped with strips of red pepper or chard (photo left)

conill amb cebes – pieces of rabbit meat in an onion-vegetable jus

ensaimada – Yeast pastry roll sprinkled with icing sugar; often copied but nowhere as good as on the Balearics

frit mallorquí – chopped innards and vegetables – with a lot of garlic and fennel par for the course

gató amb gelat d'ametlla – the most popular island dessert: a fluffy almond cake with almond ice cream

llom amb col – cabbage roulade with pork or young pigeon in a jus made from wine, bacon, raisins and pine nuts

pa amb oli – (pronounced "pambóli") – slices of bread are rubbed with the flesh of the hard-skinned *remallet* tomato, olive oil and salt on top – and hey presto!

panades – pasties with a lamb filling (served at Easter in particular)

porcella – roast piglet

sobrassada – soft, raw paprika sausage, tastes best well-aged

sopas mallorquines – no soup actually, but a cabbage-and-pork stew on thin slices of bread, *sopas*, previously dried in the sun

trempó – typical summer salad made with diced tomatoes, onions and green pepper in olive oil

tumbet – vegetable stew made from slices of potato, aubergine and red pepper, topped with tomato sauce

variat – The Mallorcan version of tapas: colourful mix of different nibbles, with round, salty *galletes d'oli* biscuits on the side

and creativity. Many restaurants offer tasting menus or menus of the day that give a good impression of the local cuisine and are less expensive than dining à la carte.

The qualities of Mallorcan olive oil have long been known, but these days, many ingredients that the locals pop into their traditional clay pots are growing in popularity. Typical *vegetables* in the island's cuisine include chard, which is used in dishes such as *cocarroi:* turnovers that are sold in local bakeries. Cabbage is used in Mallorcan restaurants in dishes such as *llom amb col;* chick peas are cooked into stews and aubergines are used to make the vegetable dish *tumbet.* And of course, generous portions of onions are a must. Popular *meat dishes* include oven-roasted lamb or suckling pig, as well as rabbit and pork, prepared as a sausage or as tenderloin. *Fish* is served in a salt crust or under a bed of vegetables, and squid is prepared with onions. Mushroom stews and a range of different rice dishes are also popular. Ingredients such as fennel, parsley, bell pepper and garlic provide the necessary zest.

As a region of Spain, Mallorca is of course wine country, even though beer *(cerveza)* is gaining ground. Over the past few years, *Mallorcan wines* were able to recoup their good reputation gained over centuries before the grapes were destroyed by the phylloxera bug at the end of the 19th century.

Most Mallorcan red wines are pressed from the Manto Negro grape. Wine aficionados rate wines produced by the *Bodegas José L. Ferrer* (see p. 100) in Binissalem and *Macía Batle* from Santa Maria. Mallorcans drink wine in modest quantities at both lunch and dinner, usually complemented at the table by a bottle of water *(aigo/agua)* with *(amb/con)* or without *(sense/sin) gas,* i.e. sparkling or still. A refreshing drink in the summer months is *horchata d'ametlla* (almond milk). For their breakfast, the locals will order a *café con leche* (milky coffee), and after a meal a *café* (espresso) or a *cortado* (espresso with milk). The bubbly is known as *cava* and liqueurs as *chupito. Salut!*

Mallorcans enjoy their wine most when it's served with food

Good restaurants usually require a reservation; at arrival, when you enter the restaurant, the maître d' or waiter will show you to your table. The bill is usually presented folded on a small plate, on which you can later leave the tip. Holidaymakers are often surprised to see that the olives that are nearly always served unasked sometimes appear on the bill, as well as the *cubierto.* Add to this the IVA (VAT, Value Added Tax).

SHOPPING

Mallorcan flair for your home: Toss your salads with fine oils and herb salts from the island, and serve them with olivewood cutlery, complemented with a glass of organic wine. Other lovely souvenirs include ceramics and linens.

ART

Nearly 3000 painters are said to live and work here. The most famous is Miquel Barceló, but Bernardí Roig, Susy Gómez, Amparo Sard and Guillem Nadal are also internationally successful. The galleries *Pelaires* (see p. 40), *Kewenig (C/Sant Feliu)*, *Fran Reus (Passeig de Mallorca 4)* and *Xavier Fiol (C/ Sant Jaume 23a)* in Palma regularly exhibit surprising works by local artists at various prices. You can get the best overview of local art during the *Nit de l'Art* gallery night on the third weekend of September in Palma.

FASHION

Many of Mallorca's talented fashion designers have shops in Palma, such as Rosa Esteve alias *Cortana (C/ Can Asprer 1)*, *Tolo Crespí (C/ Arabí 3)* or *Xisco Caimari (C/ Malaga 41)*. Spanish designers are particularly creative when it comes to elegant party dresses and ball gowns. The best streets to shop around for this kind of thing in the capital, Palma, are Passeig des Born, Jaume III, and Carrer San Miguel. The *Festival Park* (see p. 43) outlet centre offers affordable shoes, fashion and sporting kit from local and international brands. Make sure to try on any garment however: a Spanish size 42 is the equivalent of a British size 14!

FOOD & DRINK

The incomparable *ensaimadas* are yeasty pastry rolls sold with or without filling. In supermarkets you will find *hierbas,* the bright green herbal aniseed liqueur, as well as a black sweet herbal liqueur by the name of *palo*. The only (mild) island brandy is called *Suau*. Delicious INSIDER TIP *Mel de na Marta* comes from Artà. Marta sells her honey – mainly from live oak and carob blossoms – at the weekly markets in Pollença *(Sun)*, Sineu *(Wed)*, and Artà *(Tue)*, as well as in health food shops.. *Tàperes* (capers) are primarily cultivated in the south of Mallorca around Campos and Felanitx. The buds of the pink-and-white caper plant are marinated in a vinegar-and-oil

Made in Mallorca: there's no need to buy kitsch souvenirs to remind you of your holiday on the largest Balearic island

brine. They are sold at weekly markets in any quantity you like, as are olives. The small green, bitter ones grow on the island, while the large ones are usually imported from Andalucia. Cold-pressed olive oil from Sóller is well worth buying, there's nothing between it and the best Italian oils. All these treats are on offer in many places on the island at the *fires*, autumn fairs (see p. 131).

(see p. 131)

JEWELLERY

Tired of faux pearls? Ignore the enormous shops around Manacor and scour the weekly markets for real Mallorcan artisanal handicrafts and unique jewellery. Recommendable markets include Santanyí *(Wed)*, Campos *(Thu)* and Valldemossa *(Sun)*.

LEATHER & LINEN

Inca and neighbouring villages, as well as Llucmajor, are at the heart of a leather industry that is once again flourishing. It is worth looking out for shoes in particular, as they are relatively cheap to buy. Traditional decorative fabrics with a distinctive tongue pattern called by the Malay name *ikats* are still woven in Santa Maria and in Pollença. The heavy linen fabrics *(robes de llengo)* are labour-intensive to produce, hence not that cheap. You can buy by the yard, or sets, pillow cases and blankets.

POTTERY

To cook like the islanders, you'll need traditional *greixoneras* and *olles:* brown clay pots that are standard in every Mallorcan kitchen. Pòrtol and Felanitx are known for their ceramics. Little bowls or plates in modern designs are perfect souvenirs; the pottery makers will pack them carefully to ensure they won't break in transit. The ceramics fair *Fira de Fang* takes place in Marratxí in March.

PALMA & SURROUNDS

MAP INSIDE THE BACK COVER
(151 E–F4) (⚲ E–F7) One of the things that makes Palma so fascinating to both locals and foreigners is that this town is both old and young.

Its lively inner city is the undisputed heart of Mallorca. Here and in the adjoining districts is where almost half of the island residents – about 400,000 people – live. And this is also where all the traffic converges. In order to be able to enjoy the ambience of the city properly, it is better to leave the car in one of the blue parking zones or in an underground car park (see p. 135). City hall has been working to reduce traffic within the city. For this reason, only residents may drive and park in many of the alleyways that make up the maze of one-way streets. Stroll through one of the largest preserved medieval cities of the Mediterranean, once an important hub for the trading and warring powers of the region. Its former – and thanks to tourism, also current – affluence is tangible almost everywhere. And everything is in close proximity: the peaceful inner courtyards of sumptuous noblemen's palaces are next door to busy street cafés surrounded by surging traffic; dark, incense-scented churches can be found next to the bustling activity under the bright lights of the market halls; squares bathed in cheery sunlight are situated next to shady arcades.

The city guides of INSIDER TIP ▶ *Mallorca Rutes (C/ Morei 7 | tel. 9 71 72 89 83 | www.mallorcarutes.es | Mon–Sat 10am–3pm)* can tell you where the city's history

Photo: La Seu Cathedral

Mallorca's heart beats down on the left-hand side of the island – the prettiest town in the Mediterranean draws visitors as well as locals

CITY WHERE TO START?
(U C6) (*⌀ c6*)
Start your walking tour at **La Seu Cathedral,** then cross through the upper Old Town via Plaça Major, Plaça Espanya, the historic quarter and Plaça Llotja to the harbour. Parking: the car park on Parc de la Mar directly below the cathedral. Bus: take the city bus EMT (line 15) to Plaça de la Reina.

is especially exciting. One of the walking tours they offer leads through the Jewish district *(duration 1.5 hrs / 15 euros)*. Palma may not be a Gaudí city like Barcelona, but you will also see architecture in the Spanish Art Nouveau style here. Get a folding map with tour recommendations at *Arca,* the Association for the Revitalisation of Old Centres *(C/ de Can Oliva 10)*. The number 50 red double-decker buses stop at all the tourist attractions. One non-stop round trip takes about 90 minutes. The 24-hour ticket *(21 euros incl.*

The Art Nouveau exterior of the Gran Hotel

wine and tapas) lets you hop on and off at any of the 18 stops as often as you want between 9:30 am and 8 pm. You can explore Palma more economically and away from the main tourist routes by taking the municipal buses. The number 2 bus route leads around the city centre, number 7 departs from the villas in Son Vida and ends in the migrant district of Son Gotleu *(single journey 1.50 euros | www.emtpalma.es)*.

SIGHTSEEING

ES BALUARD ★ (U A4) *(⌂ a4)*
This modern building fits in brilliantly with Palma's historic fortifications, forming a fascinating contrast to the contemporary Spanish and international artworks. Great views of port and cathedral can be had from the ☼ roof terraces.

Plaça Porta de Santa Catalina 10 | www. esbaluard.org | Tue–Sat 10am–8pm, Sun 10am–3pm | admission 6 euros, free on public holidays (informative English-language audio guide), for further reductions see website

BANYS ARABS ● (U D6) *(⌂ d6)*
Arabic baths – well, strictly speaking, the plural is wrong, as all that is left to see is a dome and pillars with various 10th-century capitals. The gardens are a good spot for relaxation; gardens and baths belong to the *Font i Roig* palace, connected by a bridge. *C/ de Serra 7 | daily 9am–7pm | admission 2 euros*

CASTELL DE BELLVER ☼ (151 E4) *(⌂ E7)*
Sturdy and defensive from the outside, rather elegant in its circular interior courtyard framed by loggias, the royal castle dominates the town. Begun under Jaume I and completed in 1309, it served only briefly as a residence for Jaume II, later as a dungeon and a place of terrible pogroms against the Jewish population (14th century). Today, the castle houses the historical museum. The courtyard is used for concerts. The view of the city and port alone makes the drive up worthwhile. *Mon 8:30am–1pm, April–Sept Tue–Sat 8:30am–8pm, Sun 10am–8pm, Oct–March Mon–Sat 8:30am–6pm, Sun 10am–6pm | admission 4 euros, Sun free*

CONVENT DE SANT FRANCESC (U E5) *(⌂ e5)*
The highlights of the otherwise fairly sober church facade are the rose window and the Baroque portal. The interior of the large 17th-century basilica shelters a magnificent Baroque altar, as well as the tomb of philosopher and missionary Ramón Llull. The monastery building with its beautiful Gothic cloisters is home

to a school. *Plaça Sant Francesc 7 | Mon–Sat 9:30am–12:30pm and 3:30–6pm, Sun 9:30am–12:30pm | admission 1 euro*

FUNDACIÓ PILAR I JOAN MIRÓ ★
(151 E4) (*Ⓜ E8*)

Following the wishes of Joan Miró (1893–1983), a Catalan by birth and a Mallorcan by choice, the artist's studio and residence were converted into a "place where people live, create and talk together". Part of Miró's bequest can be seen in the museum building which has been designed beautifully by Rafael Moneo; there are also changing exhibitions. Don't miss the park and the café with a wall mosaic! At certain times, Miró's studio is also open to visits. *C/ Saridakis 29 | Cala Major | miro.palmademallorca.es | Tue–Sat 10am–7pm, in winter 10am–6pm, Sun 10am–3pm | ● admission 7.50 euros, Sat from 3pm, 1st Sun in the month and on open days (see website) free*

ART NOUVEAU BUILDINGS

In Palma some beautifully restored facades show the Catalan version of Art Nouveau, *modernisme*. To name but a few: *Edifici Casayas* on Plaça Mercat, built in 1908–11 by Francesc Roca. Diagonally opposite, on Plaça Weyler, arguably the city's most beautiful Art Nouveau facade: the ★ *Gran Hotel (Mon–Sat 10am–8pm, Sun 11am–2pm | admission 4 euros)*, built in 1901–03 by Lluís Domenec i Montaner, today an art gallery with restaurant. Standing next to each other on the Plaça Marqués de Palmer, the houses *Can Rei* and *L'Aguila* were built in 1908–09 and are famous for their colourful mosaics. It is here that the influence of the great master of Catalan *modernisme,* Antoni Gaudí, makes itself felt the most. In contrast, *Can Corbella* in Carrer Jaume II shows Moorish influence.

LA SEU CATHEDRAL ★ (U C6) (*Ⓜ c6*)

The most famous building on the island seems to sit above the sea not unlike a protective mother hen. From the outside, the church doesn't begin to convey the height and light it displays inside. The main nave, some 110 m/120 yds long, boasts 14 slim pillars, just under 22 m/72 ft high and the large rose window in the main apse (11.5 m/37.7 ft in diameter), made up from 1236 pieces of glass, transforms the rays of the sun into a colourful spectacle. Another enchanting sight is the Gaudí chandelier above the altar – and the "Feeding of the 5000" in St Peter's Chapel, a giant ceramic work by the Mallorcan artist Miquel Barceló. Visitors are now able to explore the 🔆 INSIDER TIP roof *(admission 12 euros, sign up on the website)* from April to October and enjoy a breathtaking

---

MARCO POLO HIGHLIGHTS

★ **Es Baluard**
Modern art in the former citadel with great views over the city → 34

★ **Fundació Pilar i Joan Miró**
Memorial and museum in the artist's former residence → p. 35

★ **Gran Hotel**
Splendid example of Art Nouveau restoration in Palma → p. 35

★ **La Seu Cathedral**
Most beautiful composition of light and stone in the Mediterranean → p. 35

★ **Port de Portals**
Little Marbella: a place to see and be seen → p. 45

view over the city and ocean from there. *Plaça Almoina | www.catedraldemallorca. info | Mon–Fri June–Sept 10am–6:15pm, April/May and Oct 10am–5:15pm, Nov– March 10am–3:15pm, Sat 10am–2:15pm | admission 7 euros*

MUSEU DE MALLORCA (U C6) (📖 c6)

During the 13th century, long before tourism, Mallorca became a major centre in the Western Mediterranean. At the Museu de Mallorca you will learn just what this meant for the lives of the islanders. After ten years of renovations, the museum with 400 pieces from eight centuries has once again opened its doors. *C/ Sa Portella 5 | Tue–Fri 10am–6pm, Sat/Sun 11am–2pm | admission 2.40 euros*

PALAUS (PALACES)

Most of the palaces of the local bourgeoisie and nobility, usually erected in the 15th and 16th centuries in the Italian style, can be found in the Old Town around the cathedral and in Sa Portella. These buildings are characterised by sober, fortress-like facades and cheerful patios (inner courtyards) full of flowers. The palaces are normally not open to the public. However, some allow the occasional glimpse. Particularly beautiful is the *Can Marqués (C/ Zanglada 2 | Mon–Sat 10am–3pm | admission 6 euros)* which still retains its original décor from around 1900. Easy to visit and free: ● *Casal Solleric (Passeig des Born 27 | www.casasolleric.palma.cat | Tue–Sat 11am–2pm and 3:30–8:30pm, Sun 10am– 2:30pm)* which has been converted into an art gallery and café. The best time to visit the palaces is INSIDER TIP ▶ the week around Corpus Cristi (a moveable feast) where about a third of the overall 154 town palaces open their patio. Some of them put on concerts at that time too *(for more information, check with the tourist offices).*

PALAU MARCH MUSEU ●
(U C5) (📖 c5)

In 2003, the descendants of legendary banker Joan March opened their town palace to the public, to display an impressive collection of artworks, amongst them a Neapolitan nativity scene with over 1000 figures and other parts. The ground floor houses a pretty branch of the Cappuccino chain of coffee houses. *C/ Palau Reial 18 | www.fundacionbmarch.es | Mon–Fri 10am–6:30pm (in winter 10am–2pm), Sat 10am–2pm | admission 4.50 euros*

PALAU DE S'ALMUDAINA
(U C 5–6) (📖 c5–6)

Seen from the sea, the cathedral and the royal palace appear like one and the same building. The former alcázar of the emir, later a residence of the Aragonese kings, today houses the military headquarters and accommodates King Felipe VI when he spends time on Mallorca. The highlights of the palace are the royal chambers and the Gothic chapel of Santa Ana. *C/ Palau Reial 10 | daily summer 10am– 8pm, winter 10am–6pm | admission 7 euros (Wed and Thu summer 5–8pm, winter 3–6pm free!), guided tour 4 euros*

PLAÇAS (SQUARES)

Just sit down and look around with a cup of coffee or a glass of wine: this is the favourite pastime of locals and visitors alike on Palma's squares, such as the *Plaça de Cort* (U D5) (📖 d5), the pedestrianised town hall square with the olive tree that has been standing here in front of the *ajuntament* for several hundred years. Or the stock-exchange square �▲ *Plaça Llotja* (U B5) (📖 b5), with views of the former maritime stock exchange from the 15th century and the port. The pretty rectangular *Plaça Major* (U D4) (📖 d4), the main square in the upper town, framed by yellow-painted facades of houses and ar-

The impressive olive trees on Plaça de Cort are several hundred years old

cades, is almost completely in the hands of tourists. In the cafés on the *Plaça Espanya* (U E2) *(∭ e2)*, the locals tend to be left to themselves. In a swirl of pigeons Jaume I looks down from his pedestal onto this busy transport hub with the bus station and terminus of the Sóller railway. Around the corner, housewives and foodies meet at *Plaça de l'Olivar* (U E3) *(∭ e3)*, before or after the shopping in the *Mercat d'Olivar,* the town's largest market hall – not without looking in at INSIDERTIP *Cervecería Anfos (market hall stall no. 7 | tel. 9 71 72 91 20)*: Trini and Manolo can fry the fish or meat you've bought on the market. The place where everybody fetches up at one stage or another is the *Plaça Rei Joan Carles* (U B–C4) *(∭ b–c4)* with a turtle obelisk in its centre, the usually busy *Bar Bosch* and *Café Solleric*.

PORT (U A–B 5–6) *(∭ a–b 5–6)*

The fishing port is limited by the long jetty reaching out into the sea below the cathedral. This is also where the ships leave for the one-hour ● *Cruceros Marco Polo* cruises around the harbour *(www.crucerosmarcopolo.com | March–Oct Mon–Sat hourly 11am–4pm | 12 euros per person);* a refreshing and relaxing change for visitors whose feet need a break.

FOOD & DRINK

Starting at 8 pm, the entire district of INSIDERTIP *Santa Catalina* is transformed into an open-air buffet with international offerings. There are many restaurants to choose from in the traffic-calmed *Carrer Fábrica*. In the summer, its sidewalks are packed with tables. Recommended in Santa Catalina: the vegetarian *La Golondrina (C/ Sant Magí 60 | www.lagolondrina.bar)* and the Spanish-Mediterranean cuisine of *Bros (C/ Cotoner 54 | www.brospalma. com)*. *Simply Delicious (Plaça Navegació 5)* are the Middle Eastern dishes served in the restaurant of the same name. Always

rectly next to the fish market (Sa Llotja des Peix). *C/ Contramuelle | Es Mollet | tel. 9 71 72 11 82 | www.caneduardo.com | daily from 1:30pm, Nov–Feb closed Sun afternoons | Moderate*

CAN MIQUEL (U B4) (🏛 b4)

The established ice cream parlour offers a divinely large selection of ice cream flavours at its two stores at *Carrer Montcades 9* and *Avinguda Jaume III 6*. In the winter, the enjoyment continues with pastries and chocolates and a sip or two of tea or coffee – all the parlour's house blends, of course. *Daily from 9am | www.facebook.com/canmiquel1979*

MERCADO GASTRONÓMICO SAN JUAN (151 E4) (🏛 F7)

The market in the former slaughterhouse S'Escorxador has blossomed into a tapas meeting point. You can choose from among 17 stands! The place is packed at the weekend. Very Spanish ambience. *C/ de l'Emperadriu Eugènia 6 | www.mercadosanjuanpalma.es | daily from 12:30pm | Budget*

ES MOLLET ✲ (151 F4) (🏛 F7)

A gifted chef magics up the most wonderful grilled fish, to be enjoyed with views of the small port of Es Molinar/Portixol in the east of Palma – at fairytale prices however. *Tel. 9 71 24 71 09 | www.restauranteesmollet.com | closed Sun | Expensive*

RESTAURANT PALMA TENNIS (151 E4) (🏛 F7)

They know how to do it: the Swedish owners of the hotels Portixol in Palma and Espléndido in Port de Sóller have now also opened a sports centre with an exclusive, vintage-style restaurant. Here, you can enjoy light and healthy cuisine. A set menu costs 17 euros. *C/ Joan Maria*

The name is misleading: Simply Fosh

packed, the bar *Can Frau (Santa Catalina market hall | Plaça de la Navegació)* has been serving classic tapas for 50 years.

13 % (U B4) (🏛 b4)

This lower ground floor eatery offers good food and good value. Fresh colours dominate the decor, the small Mediterranean dishes are tasty. Set lunch menu! *C/ Feliu 13 | a side street of Passeig des Born | www.13porciento.com | closed Sun | Budget*

CAN EDUARDO (U A5) (🏛 a5)

One of the best restaurants for fish, mussels and seafood in Palma. Located di-

Thomás 4 | near the Santa Catalina quarter | tel. 9 71 28 20 00 | daily | Moderate

SIBILLA (U D1) (*ffl d1*)

Should you be overcome by hunger while shopping on the pedestrianised promenade of Blanquerna, then the Sibilla is the place to go. The interior of the restaurant is simple and modern, and you can enjoy breakfast, lunch and dinner there at affordable prices (set menu around 10 euros). *C/ de Blanquerna 7 | tel. 9 71 20 10 03 | daily | Budget*

SIMPLY FOSH ⊙ (U D3) (*ffl d3*)

Slow Food Michelin-starred chef Marc Fosh and his team use seasonal products to create stunning dishes that are anything but simple, and serve them in their patio restaurant in the exclusive *Convent de la Missió* hotel, decorated in light and fresh colours. The three-course INSIDER TIP set lunch menu costs only 19.50 euros. *C/ Missió 7a | tel. 9 71 72 01 14 | www.simplyfosh.com | closed Sun | Moderate–Expensive*

SHOPPING

Ready for a little shopping spree? First, you must stroll along the stately boulevard *Passeig des Born* and up and down *Jaume III.* If you're up for more, walk up *Carrer Unió* and turn down *Carrer Sant Miguel,* passing Palma's best fashion shops as you go. You will find shops stocked with international designer brands such as Gaultier, Prada or Dolce & Gabbana as well as boutiques featuring the creations of Spanish designers (Ángel Schlesser, Adolfo Domínguez, Purificación García, Sita Murt, El Ganso, Mar Sobrón and Custo). Pretty ballerinas by Jaime Mascaró or shoes from Camper are cheaper here than at home. Popular chain stores such as Zara and Man-

go have also opened up stores so you're sure to find something to buy whatever your budget may be.

SES 3 MARIES (U D4) (*ffl d4*)

At the three Marys, you can buy decorative art and food souvenirs from the island: organic olive oils, spicy sauces, fig beer, ceramics, raffia totes – everything in guaranteed high quality. *C/ de la Pescateria 2 | www.facebook.com/sestresmaries | Mon–Sat 10am–8pm*

BON DINAR (U D2) (*ffl d2*)

Good fine foods shop selling Mallorcan specialities and wines. *C/ San Miguel 75 | Mon–Fri 9am–5pm, Sat 10am–1pm*

CAFÈS LLOFRIU (U E3) (*ffl e3*)

Sniff and taste your way through more than 30 different kinds of coffee! The café has been freshly grinding its beans right across from the gourmet market Mercat d'Olivar since 1866. You absolutely must try the house blend. *C/ Josep Tous i Ferrer 10*

CENTRE DE MODA (U C3) (*ffl c3*)

Fashion designer Tolo Crespí and hair stylist Carlos Martín set up a place for holistic beauty and nutritional advice here. *C/ Arabí 3 | www.tolocrespi.es*

COLMADO SANTO DOMINGO (U C5) (*ffl c5*)

Photogenic little shop in Palma's historic quarter selling *sobrasadas, jamón serrano* and other specialities. *C/ Santo Domingo 1*

ESPECIAS CRESPI (U E4) (*ffl e4*)

Oriental aromas emerge from Mallorca's most famous spice shop. Over 150 different types of herbs and spices are sold by the packet, from basic oregano to expensive *azafrán* (saffron). *Via Sindicato 64*

SA FORMATGERIA (U C2) *(𝄽 c2)*

This tiny shop creates a great stink, in the best possible way: just follow the aromas of countless Mediterranean cheeses wafting out the door. Bar and shop at the same time, with affordable degustation plates and good wines. INSIDER TIP ▶ *Tabla mallorquina* with six local cheeses to try (8.50. euros)! *C/ Oms 30 | www.safor matgeria.com*

ART GALLERIES

The art scene on the island is vibrant and colourful. Here's a selection from over 30 relevant addresses in Palma: *Altair (C/ Sant Jaume 23); Casal Solleric (Passeig des Born 27); Sa Nostra (C/ Concepció 12); Sala Pelaires (C/ Pelaires 23).* The island's largest arts event takes place in September: the INSIDER TIP ▶ *Nit de l'Art.* A whole night is dedicated to the arts – in about 25 galleries, plus live music in the streets and a variety of culinary treats.

MERCADILLO ECOLÓGICO ⊛
(U C2) *(𝄽 c2)*

The weekly market selling exclusively organic produce. *Plaça Obispo Berenguer de Palou | Tue/Sat 8am–2pm*

TABACOS ROIG (U C4) *(𝄽 c4)*

Toni Roig's well-stocked tobacco shop is already a legend. Look no further for the world's most famous cigars, sold much cheaper than at home. *Passeig des Born 20*

ENTERTAINMENT

The cathedral, the castle and the harbour boulevard are lit up when the nightlife shifts up a gear after midnight in the *Sa Llotja* quarter, on the *Passeig Marítim* and in the *El Terreno* quarter. Whether your preference is just strolling around or being chauffeured from club to club

by taxi – Palma's night scenery is bright and colourful.

BAHIA JAZZ CLUB ♫ (151 E4) *(𝄽 e4)*

Relax while listening to jam sessions and live concerts and looking out over the yacht harbour from the club's panoramic terrace. *Paseo Mediterraneo 33 | 5th floor | Thu–Sat from 9pm*

LA BODEGUITA DEL MEDIO
(U B5) *(𝄽 b5)*

From Palma to Havana in just one second: grab a Mojito and dive into the crowd! Salsa and Latino is danced here non-stop and up close. *C/ Valseca 18 | from midnight*

CINE CIUTAT ●

Film buffs have established a cooperative to keep this arthouse cinema going. This is quite fortunate for visitors from abroad as well, because the cinema shows excellent films in their original language (usually with Spanish sub-

Sun off, party mood on: the nightlife on Palma begins when the blazing summer sun goes down

titles). *C/ de l'Emperadriu Eugènia 6 | www.cineciutat.org | admission 7.50 euros, Mon 5 euros*

COCO LA NUIT (U D2) (*m d2*)

Fabulous transvestite show in extravagant ambience; the food doesn't quite convince. *C/ Sant Miguel 79 | for tickets tel. 9 71 72 80 54 | from 9pm*

JAZZ VOYEUR CLUB (U B5) (*m b5*)

It may be tiny, but it's home to Palma's best live jazz. *C/ Apuntadores 5 | www.jazzvoyeurfestival.com | from midnight*

MADE IN BRASIL
(151 E4) (*m E7*)

Hot, packed, in your face: how about a marathon of samba, rumba and pop music? *Passeig Marítim 21 | from 11pm*

OPIO
(U B5) (*m b5*)

This bar all in white forms part of the Puro Design Hotel. Monday to Friday between 6 and 10pm, small snacks are served with each drink. Wednesday to Saturday between 10pm and 2am a fine DJ gets those party feet moving. *C/ Montenegro 2*

LA ROSA VERMUTERÍA
(U C–D4) (*m c–d4*)

Vermouth fever has also hit Palma. There are 50 kinds to try at the Vermutería La Rosa – sample some together with the classic Gilda skewers (olive, red pepper, anchovies). However, do not stay to have a meal – the food at the large restaurant is not to be recommended. *C/ Rosa 5 | www.facebook.com/larosavermuteria | noon–midnight*

TITO'S ☂
(151 E4) (*m E7*)

Legendary and pretty loud super-club boasting a glass elevator (and harbour views). *Passeig Marítim | www.titosmallorca.com | from midnight | admission 12–20 euros*

ALMUDAINA HOTEL ☆ (U B4) *(𝕄 b4)*
Centrally located hotel, restored a few years ago, with rooftop terrace and fabulous views of town and port. *78 rooms | Av. Jaume III 9 | tel. 9 71 72 73 40 | www.ho telalmudaina.com | Moderate*

BORN (U C4) *(𝕄 c4)*
This centrally located hotel operates from a restored 16th-century townhouse with a quiet patio. *29 rooms | C/ Sant Jaume 3 | tel. 9 71 71 29 42 | www.hotelborn.com | Budget–Moderate*

LOW BUDGET

Travellers wanting to save the admission charge at Palma's cathedral may enter at ● Mass for free, but have to refrain from walking around. *Mon–Fri 9am, Sat 9am, 7pm, Sun and public holidays 9am, 10:30am, noon, 7pm*

They still exist, the *chiringuitos,* simple beach shacks offering a limited menu. The *Bugambilia (Ctra. Andratx 29 | Cas Catalá | Caló des Macs | near the Hotel Maricel | tel. 9 71 40 27 41 | closed Nov–April)* has 20 tables directly on the water and serves a simple breakfast as well as paella, hamburgers or salads for lunch and dinner. Set menu approx. 15 euros.

A night at the *Hostal Apuntadores C/ Apuntadores 8 | tel. 9 71 71 34 91 | www.apuntadoreshostal.com)* right in the vibrant Llotja quarter costs only 50 euros; a fabulous roof terrace makes up for the lack of breakfast.

CASTILLO HOTEL SON VIDA
(151 E4) *(𝕄 E7)*
If this hotel was already the height of luxury, it is even more so now after its one-year restoration. Travellers not requiring one of the 182 luxury suites or rooms nor their own butler should still take advantage of the INSIDER TIP unique beautiful views of Palma from the ● ☆ terrace of this exclusive establishment. Your coffee will be served to right royal standards. *C/de la Raixa 2 | Son Vida | tel. 9 71 60 60 29 | www.hotelsonvida.com | Expensive*

CORONA (151 E4) *(𝕄 E7)*
Long-established guesthouse with garden and art nouveau flair in the slightly down-at-heel El Terreno quarter, particularly suited to younger people; quiet location. *10 rooms | C/ Josep Villalonga 22 | tel. 9 71 73 19 35 | www.hostal-corona. com | Budget*

INSIDER TIP **HOSTAL REGINA**
(U D2) *(𝕄 d2)*
Basic but clean guesthouse with heating, without breakfast, near Plaça Espanya. Ten rooms and genial British owners. *C/ de Sant Miquel 77 | tel. 9 71 71 37 03 | www.hostalreginapalma.com | Budget*

HOSTAL RITZI (U B5) *(𝕄 b5)*
In the Apuntadores entertainment mile; basic accommodation with a pretty patio. *17 rooms | C/ Apuntadors 6 | tel. 9 71 71 46 10 | www.hostalritzi.com | Budget*

PALAU SA FONT (U B5) *(𝕄 b5)*
One of the first, and today still most affordable, boutique hotels in the city (doubles starting at 145 euros), family and pet friendly. Artists helped design the 16th century palace. You can take a dip in the small pool in the courtyard. *19 rooms | C/*

What a sight! View from the roof terrace of the Santa Clara Hotel to the convent of the same name

Apuntadores 38c | tel. 9 71 71 22 77 | www. palausafont.com | Expensive

SANTA CLARA (U D6) (*∅ d6*)

A 17th-century palace in the Santa Catalina district has been turned into a design hotel with spa and fantastic rooftop terrace. *20 rooms | C/ Sant Alonso 16 | tel. 97 17 29 23 | www.santaclarahotel.es | Moderate–Expensive*

STAY CATALINA (151 E4) (*∅ F7*)

Spend the night at one of five apartments in the trendy district of Catalina. The small hotel in a former residential building has a roof terrace and affordable long-term rates. *C/ Bayarte 14 | mobile tel. 6 01 18 28 81 | Moderate*

INFORMATION

OIT PALMA

Parc de les Estacions 1 (U E2) (∅ e2) and *Passeig del Born 27 (U B4) (∅ b4) | tel. 9 02 10 23 65 | daily 9am–8pm*

WHERE TO GO

CIUTAT JARDÍ (151 F4) (*∅ F8*)

On weekends in particular, the locals descend on this villa suburb east of Palma, and it's easy to see why: a location right by the sea with a pretty swimming beach and the "foodie mile" behind it, with INSIDER TIP excellent fish restaurants, such as *Casa Fernando (tel. 9 71 26 54 17 | closed Mon | Expensive)* serving grilled fish and seafood that restaurant guests may pick themselves at the counter. The place brings together tourists and business people. On the beach, with fabulous views of Palma Bay and food straight out of the sea, look out for the ☆ *Restaurante Bungalow (tel. 9 71 26 27 38 | closed Mon | Moderate).*

FESTIVAL PARC (152 A4) (*∅ G6*)

The fancy name hides a shopping centre with over 30 outlet stores of well-known brands as well as an entertainment centre with crazy golf, bowling, gambling halls, restaurants and 20 cinema screens. *Ctra. Palma–Inca km 7.1 | motorway exit Marratxí/Sa Cabaneta, on the left-hand side coming from Palma | www.festivalpark.es*

GENOVA (151 E4) *(⊠ E7)*

With its many authentic cosy bars and restaurants in romantic locations amongst Genova's flights of stairs and terraces, this western suburb of Palma is foodie heaven. Rustic: the *Mesón Can Pedro (tel. 9 71 70 21 62 | www.canpedro.es | daily | Budget)* with a charcoal barbecue.

PLATJA DE PALMA (152 A6) *(⊠ G8)*

This is a famous, even infamous place for watching German tourists making fools of themselves: the *Beach Club Six,* or "Ballermann", now decorated in a purist, Ibiza-chillout style, where in summer in particular the sounds of beery German joviality fill the air. Right behind it, pub after bar after pub line the *Bierstrasse* and *Schinkenstrasse* ("Beer" and "Ham Roads"),* controlled with an iron fist by the local *Bierkönig* ("King of Beer", *www.bierkoenig.com*). The best time to experience this party spectacle on the Ballermann and in Megapark is during the late afternoon happy hour. Otherwise, the sweeping 8 km (5 miles) sandy beach, divided into 16 *balnearios* (beach sections) in total, and its palm-lined promenade, is rather contemplative, were it not for the near-seamless hotels offering 43,000 beds in total. Nearly all are in the hands of tour operators, first and foremost the eight well-run establishments of the RIU chain. Nowhere on the island is the tourist infrastructure as perfect as on Platja de Palma. However, Palma's city government is keen to deal with its many superannuated hotel buildings.

The *Megapark* is a gigantic party mecca near the "Ballermann" in a neo-Gothic edifice that can fit in up to 8000 guests – now, however, the nighttime musical entertainment is all happening underground. In *S'Arenal,* right at the end of

Love at first sight: hand-woven linens at Artesania Textil Bujosa

the bay, young people can find good-value accommodation in simple guest-houses. Simple and affordable, too: the multi-storey hotel *Palma Playa (C/ Acapulco 26 | tel. 9 71 26 29 32 | www.hotelpalmaplaya-mallorca.com | Budget)*. A worthwhile change from the mostly German or international fare on Platja de Palma is on offer at *Rancho Picadero (C/Flamenco 1 | Can Pastilla | tel. 9 71 26 10 02 | daiy | Moderate)*.

PORT DE PORTALS ★ (151 E5) *(ω E8)*

The exclusive marina below Portals Nous acts like a magnet for all who want to see and be seen, including Spain's royal family; mooring fees are among the most expensive on the island. Add to the mix the harbour boulevard with its high-end boutiques and expensive restaurants. *Diablito (tel. 9 71 67 94 00 | daily | Moderate)* is mainly frequented by young people ordering huge pizzas. *Wellie's (tel. 9 71 67 64 44 | daily | Moderate)* is the (overpriced) meeting place for an evening *copa*, and serves copious salad platters. The bistro *Flanigan (www.flanigan.es | daily | Moderate)* clad in shipboards has a maritime flair. Paradoxically, the new *Beach Alm (mobile tel. 6 80 25 85 32 | www.beachalm.com | Moderate)* has been built with over 10 tons of wood from Tyrol on the white beach and turquoise bay of Portal.

5900 euros (butler and private pool included) is the rate for one summer's night charged for the Blue Oasis Suite in the *Sant Regis Mardavall Hotel (133 rooms | tel. 9 71 62 96 28 | www.mardavall-hotel.com | Expensive)*. Although freshly renovated the *Lindner Golf & Wellness Resort (tel. 9 71 70 77 77 | www.lindner.de | Expensive)* still has an African touch. Non-hotel guests may relax for the day in the ● spa for 20 euros incl. bath robe and towels.

PÓRTOL/SA CABANETA
(152 A–B4) *(ω G6–7)*

This twin village 6 km (3.7 miles) south of Santa Maria (pop. 6500) is famous for its pottery and ceramics workshops. The way to the eight *olleríes* in Pórtol, producing bellied *olles* and flat *greixoneras,* is signposted. *L'Albello (C/ Major 45 | www.ceramiquesalbello.com)* at the edge of the village has the largest selection. The workshops of *Sa Cabaneta,* hidden in the upper part of the village, are famous for their *siurell* figurines. Close to the church Sant Marçal, th *Local No 2 (C/ Casa del Poble 3 | tel. 9 71 79 79 80 | www.tapasmallorca.com | Thu–Sat from 7pm)* serves delicious tapas – the buffet almost collapses under the weight of about 50 different kinds!

SANTA MARIA DEL CAMÍ
(152 B3–4) *(ω H6)*

15 km (9.3 miles) northeast of Palma, this town of 6500 inhabitants is surrounded by the fincas of international residents. It is worth taking a look at the small 17th-century cloisters and the large *Sunday market* with ◎ organic section on the new village square. The island's organic farmers sell local fruits and vegetables as well as other products such as freshly-baked sourdough spelt bread, ostrich salami and fig jam. In the middle of the village is the craft beer brewery Sa *Nau (see p. 19)*. From here you can explore the heart of the city on foot, far away from the main thoroughfare. At the *Bar Can Beia (C/ Oleza 4)* on the old village square you really should sample the food that all Mallorcans are raised on: a serving of mixed tapas called *variat.*

There are only two linen weavers left on the island. *Artesania textil Bujosa (C/ Bernardo Santa Eugènia 53)* is the only one to still manufacture traditional *ikats* by hand; this is of course reflected in the price.

THE WEST

The steep coast of Tramuntana on the western part of the island has the most spectacular scenery on Mallorca.

If you don't have the time to enjoy the beauty of this region on a hike, you should at least drive along a section of the coastal road Ma10. While the outermost southwestern part around Andratx and Peguera has been spoiled by development, the wonderfully untouched mountain villages of Estellencs and Banyalbufar can be found hidden along the steep coast. They are accessible via long, winding roads with hairpin bends that offer surprising glimpses of old watchtowers, lemon plantations, olive groves and terrace farms along the way. The popular villages of Valldemossa, Deià and Sóller have also retained their original flair.

ANDRATX

(150 B4) *(ℳ C7)* **In the shade of a sturdy fortified church, framed by pine-covered hills, the country town of Andratx (pop. 6300) remains in a gentle snooze.** Apart from Wednesdays, when there's a market on, you won't meet many tourists here; they prefer the harbour town *Port d'Andratx* (pop. 3000), 5 km (3.1 miles) away and extremely built-up.

SIGHTSEEING

CALA LLAMP/SA MOLA

Check out the level of (nouveau) richness in such a small area! The hilly backcountry between the *Sa Mola* peninsula and

Tourist centres and the solitude of a hike: The West can offer both. And the breathtaking Serra de Tramuntana towers above it all

the steep coast above the cliff-fringed bay of *Cala Llamp* is full of breathtaking luxury villas.

CCA ANDRATX

The 43,000 square-foot space of this art gallery houses exhibitions featuring national and international contemporary art. *About half a mile outside town towards Es Capdellà | C/ Estanyera 2 | www.ccandratx. com | March–Oct Tue–Fri 10:30am–7pm, Sat/Sun until 4pm, Nov–Feb Tue–Sun 10:30am–4pm | admission 8 euros*

STUDIO WEIL

If you call ahead for an appointment, you can tour the fantastic studio designed by star architect Daniel Libeskind for the artist Barbara Weil at the end of the harbour road leading to La Mola. *Camí de Sant Carles 20 | tel. 9 71 67 16 47 | www. studioweil.com*

FOOD & DRINK

The harbour town of Port d'Andratx has one of the largest fishing fleets

Enjoying fish with a view: Restaurant Rocamar

cel. He takes care of all the details and cooks divine meals, no matter whether you order fish, vegetables or dessert. *Ctra. Port d'Andratx 67 | tel. 9 71 23 58 30 | www. oliu.es | closed Mon | Moderate– Expensive*

URBANO
Empty for some time, the former famous restaurant El Patio has been re-opened under a new name. The fine Mediterranean cuisine featuring fresh local products has earned a good reputation. *Ctra. Andratx–Port d'Andratx (Ma1), km 30.5 | tel. 9 71 67 17 03 |www.restaurante-urba no.com | daily | Moderate–Expensive*

WHERE TO STAY

CATALINA VERA
Simple, but pretty clean hostal with garden in the port area; all rooms have a balcony or terrace. *20 rooms | C/ Isaac Peral 63 | tel. 9 71 67 19 18 | www.hostal catalinavera.es | Moderate*

MON PORT HOTEL
Comfortable hotel with spa on the edge of Port d'Andratx. *139 rooms and suites | C/ Cala d'Egos | tel. 9 71 23 86 23 | www. hotelmonport.com | Moderate–Expensive*

VILLA ITALIA
Befitting the refined ambience, this 1920s villa over the port was converted into a stylish exclusive hotel with a "Castillo" extension, spa, restaurant and cocktail bar. *21 rooms and suites | Camino de San Carlos 13 | tel. 9 71 67 40 11 | www.hotelvillaitalia.com | Expensive*

WHERE TO GO

BANYALBUFAR/ESTELLENCS ★
(151 D2) (*ш D5–6*)
These two rock-solid villages of Arabic origin cling to the mountain high above

of the island. Don't even think about not having some local fish because of the – admittedly steep – prices. The ☆ restaurants *Can Pep (C/ Mateo Bosch 30a | tel. 9 71 61 95 91 | www.res taurantcanpep.com | daily | Moderate– Expensive)*, *Rocamar (Av. Almirante Riera Alemany 27 | tel. 9 71 67 12 61 | www. rocamar.eu | daily | Moderate–Expensive)*, *Barlovento (C/ Vell d'es Far 1 | tel. 9 71 67 10 49 | closed Tue | Moderate– Expensive)* or *Miramar (Av. Mateo Bosch 18 | tel. 9 71 67 19 23 | www.mir amarpuertoadratx.com | daily | Moderate– Expensive)* make the investment even more worthwhile because of the ocean view you can enjoy along with it.

OLIU
The quality of the olives that are used for the canapés says a lot about the garden restaurant of young Mallorcan Joan Por-

the sea. Situated on the bendy Ma-10 coastal road along romantic terraces dating back to Moorish times, they are best explored on foot, up some steps, down some more steps. Situated some 25 km (15.5 miles) northwest of Palma, *Banyalbufar* (pop. 590) offers several bars and restaurants which you can explore on a stroll around the upper part of the village. The classics are *Son Tomas (tel. 9 71 61 81 49 | closed Tue | Moderate)* and the *Restaurant 1661 (tel. 9 71 61 82 45 | daily | Moderate)*. At the end of July, all restaurants jointly organise a tpas weekend with live music called *Eres Negre (www.eresnegre.com)*. An idyllic place to stay in the village of *Estellencs* (pop. 400) is the Hotel *Nord (8 rooms | tel. 9 71 14 90 06 | www.hotelruralnord.com | Moderate)*. Both villages boast romantic if difficult-to-access tiny coves with waterfalls (signposted).

CAMP DE MAR (150 B5) *(𝄞 C8)*

A wooded bendy road with pretty views connects Port d'Andratx with Camp de Mar (pop. 250) 4.5 km (2.8 miles) away, which over the past few years has seen much development and become quite refined. The comfortable hotel *Gran Camp de Mar (293 rooms | tel. 9 71 23 52 05 | Moderate)*, one of the most beautiful houses in this chain, lies right on the beach of light-coloured sand. The *Dorint Royal Golfresort & Spa (tel. 9 71 13 65 65 | www.hotel-mallorca-dorint.com | Expensive)* with 162 bright, pleasant and luxurious rooms and two suites has been integrated into the *Golf de Andratx* 18-hole links (charging a steep 105 euros for the green fee).

SANT ELM (150 A4) *(𝄞 A–B7)*

The best thing about the small seaside resort of Sant Elm (pop. 250) 8 km (5 miles) west of Andratx is its tranquillity – and the view of the offshore island of ★ 🌐 *Sa Dragonera*. In summer, Sa Dragonera can be reached by the ferry *Margarita* in about 20 minutes *(tel. 6 39 61 75 45 | www.cruserosmargarita.com | Feb–Oct from 9:45am, last return Feb–March, Oct 3pm, April–Sept*

★ Valley of Sóller
Protected by mighty peaks soaring up thousands of feet and adorned by flowering trees: welcome to Orange Valley! → p. 54

★ Torrent de Pareis
A marvel of nature, no matter which trail you take to the mouth of the torrent → p. 57

★ Fornalutx
Climbing up steps is a joy in what is perhaps the most beautiful mountain village of Mallorca. The former oil mill has the answer to the riddle of the colourful roofing tiles → p. 56

★ Sa Dragonera
The place is teeming with small, tame "dragons" – are they what gave the undeveloped island its name? The nature park is certainly beautiful → p. 49

★ Banyalbufar/Estellencs
Up steps, down steps leads the path down from the idyllic villages on the slopes of the Tramuntana mountains to the divine swimming coves → p. 48

★ Valldemossa's lower village
While strolling along flower-lined streets you will find traces of a saint – and the much sought-after jam doughnuts → p. 59

MARCO POLO HIGHLIGHTS

4:50pm | 13 euros). The strictly protected islet, 4.2 km long, up to 1 km wide with natural history museum and hiking trails, is home to endemic lizards and many types of bird. From Sant Elm not one but three hiking trails lead to the monastery of *Sa Trapa* (with refuge and managed by the GOB). The cosy *Na Caragola* restaurant *(tel. 9 71 23 90 06 | closed Wed | Moderate)* with terrace above the old harbour serves good Mediterranean fare.

DEIÀ

(146 C5) (*m F4*) **Over half of the 760 registered inhabitants of this picture-perfect hill village are foreigners. In the 1920s, Deià attracted the artists; today it's wealthy finca owners.**

Hotels and restaurants have followed suit. In summer, long lines of coaches and cars try to push through the narrow street leading through the village, and the romantic pebble beach of *Cala de Deià* is overrun with visitors.

SIGHTSEEING

CHURCH HILL ⌇

Flower-bedecked alleyways and flights of steps lead up to church and cemetery, which have far-reaching views. One of the artists who found their last resting place here is the British writer Robert Graves (1895–1985). His fictionalised biography "I, Claudius" was written in Deià, where he lived for over 40 years. A small *museum (Ca n'Alluny | www.lacasaderobertgraves.org | April–Oct Mon–Fri 10am–5pm, Sat 10am–3pm, Nov, Feb–March Mon–Fri 9am–4pm, Sat 9am–noon, Dec–Jan Mon–Fir 10:30am–1:30pm | admission 7 euros)* is dedicated to him.

FOOD & DRINK/ WHERE TO STAY

S'HOTEL D'ES PUIG ⌇
Quiet hotel on the church hill befitting the romantic village scenery, with swimming pool and fabulous views from the terrace. *9 rooms | tel. 9 71 63 94 09 | www.hoteldespuig.com | Expensive*

ES RACÓ D'ES TEIX
Eat like an emperor above the roofs of Deià if you splash out on the seven-course set meal for nearly 100 euros prepared by maverick Josef Sauerschell. *C/ de sa Vinya Vella 6 | tel. 9 71 63 95 01 | www.esracodesteix.es | closed Mon/Tue | Expensive*

LA RESIDENCIA ⌇
The former manor house, framed by cascades of blossoms, with landscaped pools and dream views of the church hill, offering 53 rooms, six suites and the trendy gourmet restaurant *El Olivo*, is a first-class choice. *Tel. 9 71 63 60 46 | www.hotel-laresidencia.com | Expensive*

ENTERTAINMENT

Tourists, the in-crowd and artists – everybody meets in Deià's only bar, the INSIDER TIP *Café sa Fonda:* One of the regulars is a grandson of Robert Graves, co-organiser of the ecological arts festival 🌐 *Posidonia*. Founded in 2010, the festival aims to use the arts, music and film to connect with older cultural traditions.

WHERE TO GO

LLUC ALCARI (146 C5) (*m F4*)
This much-photographed village of natural stone above the sea only has 13 inhabitants. The largest part of the village is taken up by the hotel ⌇ *Costa d'Or*

Does your photo finger also start to itch when you look at the natural stone village of Lluc Alcari?

(40 rooms | tel. 9 71 63 90 25 | closed Nov–April | *Expensive*), with pool and sea views. In the *Bens d'Avall* restaurant *(tel. 9 71 63 23 81 | www.bensdavall. com | closed Sun evening, Mon and Dec–Feb | Expensive)* you may feast on the finest Mediterranean cuisine on an 🌿 enchanting terrace high above the sea; the way to get there is some 6 km (3.7 miles) along a bendy road (signposted) to Sóller.

SON MARROIG 🌿 (146 B5) (*ℳ E4*)
The former retirement residence of Archduke Ludwig Salvator is today a museum. The idyllic gardens alone make a visit worthwhile. With the permission of the gatekeeper you can use the private road down to the *Sa Foradada* peninsula, where the archduke anchored in 1867 with his yacht and set foot on Mallorcan soil for the first time. If you're in luck, the restaurant on the steep cliffs, *Sa Foradada (mobile tel. 6 16 08 74 99 | www.saforada-da.com | Budget–Moderate)*, is open. Be sure to order the INSIDER TIP paella prepared over a wood fire. *On the Ma10 at km 65.5 | April–Oct Mon–Sat 9am–6pm, Nov–March 9am–5pm | admission 4 euros*

PALMANOVA/ MAGALUF/ SANTA PONÇA

(151 C–D5) (*ℳ D8*) **This huge resort conglomerate consisting of Palmanova, Magaluf and Santa Ponça belongs to Calvià, whose 52,500 inhabitants form part of the island's second-largest municipality, and one of the wealthiest in Europe.**

The wealth stems from tourism and tax revenues of rich finca owners. The stacked hotels, pubs and snack bars are fairly faceless. The beaches however are long, wide and pretty. This is British partyville, with action and showparks providing entertainment.

FOOD & DRINK

CIRO'S 🌿
Long-established large restaurant, with a terrace and sea views and good Mediterranean cuisine. *Paseo del Mar 3 | Pal-*

manova | tel. 9 71 68 10 52 | www.restau rranteciros.es | daily | Moderate

LEISURE & SPORTS

JUNGLE PARC

Various levels of difficulty have to be overcome as you work your way through the tree canopy climbing course in the pine forest. Both children and adults will get their money's worth. *Av. del Rei Jaume I | Santa Ponça | www.jungleparc. es | daily 10am–5pm | admission from 14 euros*

WESTERN WATER PARK

Trumping the neighbouring Aquaparc, this lively water park has a Western show and breathtaking tower dives. *Ctra. Cala Figuera a Sa Porrasa | Magaluf | www.wes ternpark.com | daily 10am–5pm, in mid-summer until 6pm | admission 27 euros, online booking 25 euros*

LOW BUDGET

The cosy hostel *Sa Fita Backpackers (30 beds | C/ Joan Riutort 49 | tel. 9 71 61 95 91 | www.safitabackpackers. com)* in Esporles is especially attuned to the needs of hikers and athletes with their offer of low-priced multi-bed rooms.

Starting at 9pm on almost every Thursday in the summer, the bars around the village square of Bu-nyola hold concerts featuring local bands. Have a fresh beer on tap for 1.60 euros and let the open-air evening begin.

ENTERTAINMENT

The nightlife here is somewhat in line with the cut-price hotels. Youngsters go for the *BCM* superclub *(Magaluf | May–Oct daily 10pm–6am)*.

WHERE TO STAY

SON CALIU HOTEL SPA-OASIS

It's all in the name: this INSIDER TIP spa is fabulous! Although use of the spa it-self is free for hotel guests, the treat-ments cost extra, such as the Ayurvedic head massage for 64 euros. Day guests pay 20 euros per day (8am–8pm). There are 221 rooms and suites, while top ser-vice makes up for the small size of the beach. *Av. Son Caliu 8 | tel. 9 71 68 22 00 | www.soncaliu.com | Moderate–Expensive*

WHERE TO GO

PORT ADRIANO (151 C6) *(ﾉ C9)*

The cool and unadorned concrete, glass and stainless steel modern architecture of the harbour is accentuated by its lux-ury yachts and exclusive shops and res-taurants. Unfortunately, the view of the sea is blocked by a protective wall. *Follow the signs 5 km (3 miles) from motorway exit Santa Ponça | www.portadriano.com*

PEGUERA

(150 C5) (ﾉ C8) **Peguera (pop. 3900) has always been a magnet for Ger-man tourists; maybe because the resort boasts pretty hiking trails and dreamy mountain villages in its hilly back coun-try.**

The town has also gained from seeing its former thoroughfare turned into a pe-destrianised promenade. Along the *Bule-var* you will find bars and restaurants, boutiques and souvenir shops, mostly catering for German tourists. At the end of the last century, Peguera was a bastion of so-called hibernators or long-term vacationers. Today, visitors are that bit younger, and the town is now also attracting visitors on activity holidays who flock to the island's largest tennis centre or on one of the five golf courses in the vicinity. Considering the number of visitors Peguera receives, the beaches are fairly small.

FOOD & DRINK

MAR Y MAR ☆
The fish restaurant directly on the beach offers an extensive menu with fish and seafood, soups, snacks and salads together with a view of the ocean and a relaxed atmosphere. *C/ Pinaret 6 | tel. 9 71 94 62 08 | www.marymar-mallorca. com | daily | Moderate–Expensive*

ENTERTAINMENT

DISCOTECA RENDEZVOUS
Meeting point laid out in a 1960s style for more mature clubbers on Peguera's main promenade. *Daily 10pm–6am*

WHERE TO STAY

ALDEA 2 CALA FORNELLS
Designed by star architect Pedro Otzup, this slightly labyrinthine complex is located about 1.5 km (1 mile) west of Peguera high above the sea. The apartments have different views and quality ranging from excellent to middling. *85 apartments | tel. 9 71 68 61 66 | www.aldea2. com | Moderate*

VILLA ANA
One example of the many clean and simple family guesthouses in Peguera. *35*

Cala Fornells near Peguera

rooms | C/ Gaviotas 13 | tel. 9 71 68 65 08 | www.morlanshotels.com | Budget

VILLAMIL
Part of the Hesperia chain, this comfortable beach hotel has been restored several times and boasts a pretty ☆ suite with sea view on the top floor. *125 rooms | tel. 9 71 68 60 50 | www.hesperia.com | Expensive*

WHERE TO GO

GALILEA/PUIGPUNYENT ☆
(151 D3) (*ॻ D6*)
Galilea's biblical name stands for a blissful retreat. The airy terraced village (pop. 290) some 15 km (9.3 miles) northeast of Peguera serves as an idyllic second home to many foreigners whose hous-

Get on, look out, relax: the ride on the Ferrocarril de Sóller gets you in the holiday mood

es offer fine views towards the sea. Good pizza and pasta can be had in the German-owned *Trattoria Galilea (mobile tel. 6 09 60 15 40 | daily from 11am)*. The *Bar Parroquial (tel. 9 71 61 41 87 | closed Mon)* with its patio on the pretty church square is more Spanish, but less expensive.

4 km (2.5 miles) across a small pass divide Galilea and *Puigpunyent* (pop. 1400). One of the fine old estates dotted around the village has been converted by its American owner into a fairly ostentatious hotel. The *Gran Hotel Son Net (tel. 9 71 14 70 00 | www.sonnet.es | Expensive)* represents the height of luxury with six suites (the most expensive costing 1045 euros), 18 double rooms and a few holiday cottages; a gourmet restaurant complements the ensemble.

SÓLLER

(152 A1) (*⊠ G4*) The 100-year old nostalgic narrow-gauge railway connects the town of Sóller (pop. 13800) to Palma.

The 50-minute tour with the ● *Ferrocarril de Sóller (www.trendesoller.com | return ticket 22 euros)* through 13 tunnels into the ★ *Sóller Valley* is particularly charming between October and May when the oranges are ripening. The mighty peaks protect the countless orange and lemon tress growing in the valley basin and lure hikers onto the mountain paths with breathtaking views of Sóller with its elegant art nouveau houses and pretty market square. The second historic mode of transport is a tram with open wagons *(ticket 6 euros)*, which makes its gentle way from Sóller to the port, 5 km (3.1 mile) away, which today shows a new face.

For car drivers access to the town is through a tunnel with toll *(9.90 euros return, toll charges are soon to be abandoned)* or a narrow road with hairpin bends over the tunnel mountain. If you have the time, escape the toll and the bends by taking the free scenic route via Santa Maria, Valldemossa and Deià to Sóller.

SIGHTSEEING

INSIDER TIP ECOVINYASSA ⚙

More than 2500 citrus trees grow on the idyllically situated organic finca. During the tour, visitors can learn more about oranges and lemons from the displays. The tour concludes with a glass of fresh orange juice. *Ctra. Fornalutx–Sóller | www. ecovinyassa.com | Mon–Fri 10am–2pm | admission 10 euros*

JARDÍ BOTÀNIC DE SÓLLER

This Garden of Eden is located on the outskirts of Sóller: Plants from the island, from the Mediterranean and the Canary Islands are grown, exhibited and explained. *At km 30.5 along the country road between Palma and Port de Sóller | www.jardibotanicdesoller.org | March–Oct Mon–Sat 10am–6pm, Nov–Feb 10am–2pm | admission 10 euros*

OIL MILLS

Only three types of olives may be used to make the particularly pure ● *Oli de Mallorca*. The olives harvested around Sóller are considered some of the best on the island. The town possesses two *tafonas* (oil mills) that admit visitors. The *Oli d'Oliva Verge* is produced by the *Cooperativa Agrícola Sant Bartomeu (www.cooperativasoller.com)* on the road from Sóller to Fornalutx. You can buy food souvenirs at the visitors' centre of the cooperative *Capvespre (www.centrecapvespre.com)* and take part in a guided tour of the valley's olive and orange growers. The tours are offered in a number of languages.

FOOD & DRINK

The quality of the restaurants on the harbour boulevard varies and the prices are often exorbitant. However, if you still want to eat with an ocean view, go to the

🥄 *Sa Barca (Passeig Es Través 19 | tel. 9 71 63 99 43 | closed Nov–March | Moderate–Expensive)* or 🥄 *Randemar (Passeig Es Través 16 | tel. 9 71 63 45 78 | www. randemar.com | closed Nov–mid March | Moderate–Expensive)*.

SA FÀBRICA DE GELATS

The fame of this ice-cream producer ranges far and wide. Over 40 flavours, a pretty patio. *Opposite the market hall*

ES FARO 🥄

Directly next to the lighthouse La Moleta, you can have a delicious meal high over the ocean. An extraordinary experience. Speciality: grilled red prawns. *Cap Gros de Moleta | Port de Sóller | tel. 9 71 63 37 52 | www.restaurantesfaro.es | daily | Moderate*

SA TEULERA

Real Mallorcan food for a fair price – no matter whether you decide to try the suckling pig, for example, or the set menu of the day. The Sa Teulera has been renovated, but remains rustic. *Ctra. Sóller–Puig Major | direction Fornalutx | tel. 9 71 63 11 11 | www.sateulera.es | daily | Moderate*

SHOPPING

On the narrow shopping street *C/ de sa Lluna*, you can find well-stocked retailers offering leather goods *(No. 46)*, shoes *(No. 17)*, clothing *(No. 28)*, ceramics *(No. 27)* or delicious pastries *(No. 7)*. Be sure to buy some of the INSIDER TIP Sóller Chutney at Colmado La Luna (No. 3)!

WHERE TO STAY

HOTEL ESPLÉNDIDO

The elegant vintage hotel, which is run by Swedes, is creative in its design and located directly on the ocean boulevard. The buffet is quite delicious. *70 rooms | Es Través 5 | Port de Sóller | tel. 9 71 63 18 50 | www.esplendidohotel. com | Expensive*

JUMEIRAH ⌇⌇

To spend a moment in the lap of luxury: the hotel is perched like an aerie on top of the cliffs of the harbour; you can enjoy an ocean view from practically all sides. You just want to take a look? You can do so in the INSIDER TIP *Sunset Sushi Lounge (Wed–Sun 5pm–1am)* with panorama windows. *121 rooms | C/ Bélgica | Port de Sóller | tel. 9 71 63 78 88 | www. jumeirah.com | Expensive*

WHERE TO GO

BUNYOLA (146 C5–6) (⌖ F5)

Expect an idyllic village without any major sightseeing highlights if you take a trip to Bunyola (pop. 6230). The ● village square is the lively centre of the village. Here you can get delicious take-out at *Els Fogons de Plaça (next to the town hall | tel. 9 71 14 84 92 | daily 9am–4pm)* and the mini-restaurant behind the church, *Antic Grill (C/ Santa Bàrbara 3 | tel. 8 71 03 40 07 | closed Mon/Tue | Moderate)* serves grilled fish and meat. Marion Hässler from Germany runs the organic shop ◉ *Herbes i Paraules (C/ Sant Mateu 4 | www.herbesiparaules.com)* that sells almonds, wine and honey plus local fruit and vegetables if you order them ahead of time.

At the roundabout before the tunnel heading to Sóller, a serpentine road branches off that leads through olive and almond groves to the mountain pass (about a 15-minute drive) where Anette Sommer and Frank Beck run the restaurant *Dalt des Coll (Ctra. Palma Sóller, km 22 | tel. 9 71 61 53 80 | Wed–Sun 11am–5pm, dinner with reservation)*. Here, you can almost always feast on INSIDER TIP freshly baked almond cake. The pretty Arabian-style park *Jardins d'Alfabia (at km 17 on the Ma11 | www.jardinesdealfabia. com | April–Oct daily 9:30am–6:30pm, Nov–March Mon–Fri 9:30am–5:30pm, Sat 9:30am–1pm | admission summer 6.50 euros, winter 5.50 euros)* lies on the road to Sóller.

The historic ● *Raixa (at km 12 on the Ma11 | Tue–Sat 10am–3pm | admission free)* family estate has been restored by the island council and opened to the public. The huge park and the buildings were last styled by Cardinal Antonio Despuig in the 18th/19th century. It houses an exhibit on the Tramuntana Mountains World Heritage Site.

EMBALSE DE CÚBER
(147 D–E4) (⌖ G–H4)

Together with the neighbouring *Embalse de Gorg Blau* this dammed reservoir below Puig Major supplies the city of Palma with drinking water. From the reservoir's banks it is a two-hour hike up to the mountain refuge *Tossals Verds (30 sleeping spaces, restaurant | tel. 9 71 17 37 00 | closed mid-July–mid-Sept | Budget)* 540 m/1771 ft high, an ideal base for mountain walks. *12 km (7.5 miles) from Sóller in the direction of Pollença*

FORNALUTX ★ (147 D4) (⌖ G4)

Above Sóller, you will find Fornalutx (pop. 700), which has been crowned the prettiest village on Mallorca twice. Stroll through its stepped lanes lined with flowers and ochre-coloured stone houses before enjoying a freshly squeezed orange juice on the market square. What is the secret behind the painted roofing tiles in the village? Visit the *Can Xoroi (C/ de sa Font 8 | www.canxoroi.com | Fri/Sat 10:30am–1:30pm | admission free)* to find out. You can learn more about these and other idiosyncrasies and traditions of the village at the museum of local history and culture in the former oil mill. At the restaurant ⊘ *La Cuina d'en Marc (C/ Arbona Colom 6 | tel. 9 71 63 98 64 | www.lacuinadenmarc. com | closed Mon | Moderate)*, a young, creative chef transforms regional products into delightful dishes.

MIRADOR DE SES BARQUES ⚜ (147 D4) (ᗉ G4)

This enchanting viewpoint with restaurant (our tip: try the suckling pig, *Moderate*) situated above Sóller commands magnificent panoramic views of Port de Sóller. From Mirador de ses Barques a pretty but tough hiking path takes you in about four hours to *Cala Tuent* beach. This hike leads past the simple Finca *Balitx d'Avall (10 rooms| mobile tel. 6 39 71 85 06 | www.balitxdavall.com | Budget)* serving down-to-earth dishes and offering accommodation too – even in the tower.

ORIENT (152 B2) (ᗉ G5)

The remote picturesque village of Orient (pop. 9), which mainly serves second-homers, is framed by apple trees. The former monastery *L'Hermitage (20 rooms | tel. 9 71 18 03 03 | www.hermitage-hotel. com | closed Nov–March | Expensive)* today functions as a country hotel with pool, tennis court and fine restaurant.

TORRENT DE PAREIS ★ (147 E3) (ᗉ H3)

The journey is the reward en route to the mouth of the *Torrent de Pareis*. An adventurous road leads over 14 km (8.7 miles) of hairpin bends, passes narrow rock gates and opens up great sea views; a one-hour boat trip from Port de Sóller passes gigantic rocks. The challenging climbing expedition from Escorca

through the 4-km (2.5 miles) canyon of the Torrent de Pareis lasts over six hours and should only be attempted by experienced hikers. It ends at the scree-lined mouth of the wild brook, also accessible from *Sa Calobra* through two pedestrian tunnels. A seemingly sky-high rock arch opens up a view of the sea across the pebble beach as the rocks of the canyon lie behind you. Expect crowds in the restaurants and the car park (5 cents per minute!). **INSIDER TIP** Very early in the morning and after 5pm (in the summer) there is a chance to enjoy the landscape in a more relaxed way.

Taking the steps can be this beautiful: Fornalutx

The destination of hundreds of thousands of visitors every year: the charterhouse in Valldemossa

VALLDE-MOSSA

(151 E1) *(𝄞 E5)* **Coming ☀ up from Palma on the winding road, the view of the mountain village of Valldemossa (pop. 2025) will take your breath away – especially when the almond trees are in bloom.** The summer palace King Jaume II had built here was extended by his son and successor Sancho I. Today still, the narrow houses with flowering gardens, crowned by the parish church and the monastery continue to fascinate visitors.

SIGHTSEEING

FUNDACIÓ CULTURAL COLL BARDOLET

The most enchanting feature are the paintings showing dance scenes by Coll Bardolet, the Catalan painter who lived in Valldemossa up to his death in 2007. In accordance with his wishes part of his work was transferred to the art founda-

tion that bears his name. It has found a worthy home on the main street. *C/ Blanquerna 4 | www.fccollbardolet.org | Mon–Sat Nov–March 10am–4pm, April–Oct 10am–2pm and 3–7pm, Sun 10am–4pm or 8pm | admission free*

REAL CARTUJA

Every year, over 300,000 tourists shuffle through the monastery on the trail of Frédéric Chopin and George Sand who spent six cold and wet weeks here in winter 1838–39. Before half past ten and from four o'clock onwards you can admire everything in peace and quiet. From 1399 to 1835, the former royal residence was a carthusian monastery. The building we see today dates from the 18th century. The old monastic pharmacy is well worth seeing, as is the exhibition on Archduke Ludwig Salvator with pieces out of his estate and a lot of information on the life of this Mallorca enthusiast. Don't miss the *Palau de Rei Sanxo* either, for its precious furnishings and maybe a short piano concert. *www.cartujadelvalldemossa.com | Mon–*

Sat 9:30am–6:30pm (Oct–March earlier closing times), April–Oct also Sun 10am–1pm | admission 8.50 euros

VALLDEMOSSA'S LOWER VILLAGE ★

No other island village is adorned with as many flowers as Valldemossa's lower village with its Gothic parish church of Sant Bartomeu. The decorative tiles on every house depict scenes from the life of Santa Catalina, born in Carrer Rectoría. The former maidservant Catalina Tomàs (1531–74) has been honoured with a charming monument next to the parish church. Mallorcans drive for miles to see her – and buy some *cocas de patata*, potato doughnuts available in any bakery here.

FOOD & DRINK/ WHERE TO STAY

ES PETIT HOTEL VALLDEMOSSA

Treat yourself to the luxury of enjoying Valldemossa in the evening after all the day tourists have left! The small hotel at a prime location in the village centre offers eight delightfully renovated rooms. *C/ Uetam 1 | tel. 9 71 61 24 79 | www.espetithotel-valldemossa.com | Expensive*

VALLDEMOSSA ⚜

Blessed with a spectacular location on the slope of a hill and an excellent restaurant (go for the set menu!) and 12 suites, this finca hotel is a place fit for a king, including views of the Real Cartuja and the surrounding mountains. *Ctra. Vieja de Valldemossa | tel. 9 71 61 26 26 | www.valldemossahotel.com | Expensive*

WHERE TO GO

ERMITA DE LA TRINITAT ● ⚜
(151 E1) (*ш E5*)

Founded in 1648, the tiny hermitage offers terrific views of sea and coast. To-day still, hermits live here, following the rules of saints Paul and Anthony. The car is best left at the car park below; the romantic if narrow and bendy road can be tackled on foot (around 20 mins). *Around 3 km (1.9 mile) north on the Deià road, a narrow drive opposite the Can Costa restaurant*

ESPORLES (151 D–E2) (*ш E6*)

The long-drawn-out village of Esporles (pop. 4960) with its ● lively village square lies in a fertile, evergreen valley some 15 km (9.3 miles) northwest of Palma. The former post office houses the *Hostal d'Esporles (Plaza España 8 | on the church square | tel. 9 71 61 02 02 | www. hostalesporles.com | Moderate)* with ten prettily restored rooms within old walls, garden, whirlpool and in-house restaurant with regional cuisine.

Situated around 1.5 km (1 mile) north of Esporles, the country estate of *La Granja (www.lagranja.net | daily 10am–7pm, winter 10am–6pm | admission 15 euros)* dates back to Roman and Arab times. Since the 1970s the place has been an open-air museum showing workshops as well as the salons of the nobility. On Wednesdays and Fridays there are performances of regional dances and a horse show.

PORT DE VALLDEMOSSA
(151 E1) (*ш E5*)

Tiny and romantic, this pebbly harbour bay, suitable for swimming, is reached after 7 km (4.4 miles) of driving on hairpin bends (signposted turn-off from the Ma10). Visitors travelling in a large hire car and feeling a bit nervous should avoid this – the only – access road!) Try the *Es Port* beach tavern *(C/ Ponent 5 | tel. 9 71 61 61 94 | www.restaurantesport. es | Moderate)* on the nicely restored harbour.

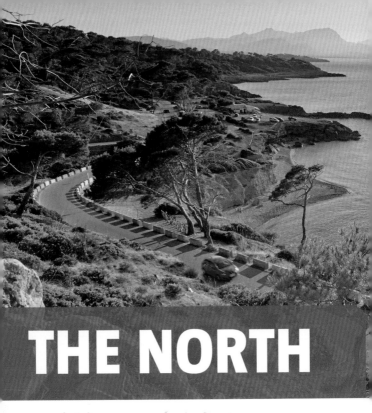

THE NORTH

Even inveterate Mallorca experts are struck speechless every time they visit the northernmost tip of the island, the Formentor peninsula. That is how surprising the constant interplay of light and colour in this largely untouched part of the island is and how astonishing the scenery around Lluc monastery, tucked away high up in the Serra de Tramuntana.

Behind every bend you will discover impressive panoramas with rugged rock faces, finca oases and a deep-blue ocean. A paradise, and not only for hikers and cyclists. The history of the Mediterranean island is still very much alive in the ancient Roman cities and medieval castles of this region. Meanwhile, modern tourist life pulses in the major tourist centres around the coves of Alcúdia and Cala Rajada.

ALCÚDIA/ PORT D'ALCÚDIA

(149 D3) (*M 2–3*) **Some say the two parts of Alcúdia (pop. 20,000) are like heaven and hell...**

The small country town, its pretty restored houses photogenically framed by a medieval town wall, and *Port d'Alcúdia*, a bit overpowering with 30,000 hotel beds stretching from the port to the Platja de Muro, then segueing seamlessly to

Photo: The small beach of S'Illot between Alcúdia and the Ermita de la Victoria

Between ancient Roman cities and medieval castles you will find exciting landscapes – and a wild natural paradise

the hotel zone. In summer, this is where it all happens, where British, German and Scandinavian tourists throng the streets, and youngsters fill the pubs and clubs every night. Compared to this, the small town of Alcúdia seems to have a near dream-like quality: cars are banned from the town centre, which allows for carefree strolling, and a large number of restaurant terraces decked out in flowers beckon guests. Prettily decorated little shops are an open invitation for some serious browsing.

SIGHTSEEING

CIUTAT DE POLLENTIA

Pollentia is the main site for Roman finds on the island. In 123 BC the Balearic Islands were conquered by the Roman consul Caecilius Metellius. Around 70 BC Pollentia was founded and became the capital of Mallorca. In 426, Pollentia was destroyed by the Vandals. The new town that rose from its ruins a little further north, under Muslim rule, was Alcúdia. Today, all that is left to see are a

The Gothic window above the entrance to Sant Jaumes

Fri 8:30pm, Sat 7:30pm, Sun 9:30am, noon, 7:30pm | admission 1 euro) with its pretty 14th-century rose window forms an integral part of the wall and received its current shape in the 16th and 19th centuries. Inside visitors can find a magnificent high altar with a statue of Saint James, and the small side chapel in Renaissance style, with the wooden *Santcrist* crucifix, which is shown every three years at the procession for the feast of Santa Ana.

TEATRE ROMÀ

Like its larger counterparts, Spain's smallest amphitheatre only managed to preserve its foundation walls. Once, 2000 people fitted in here. The tiers boast prehistoric caves, with trapezium-shaped tombs dating back to the 6th century at the entrance. *Port d'Alcúdia, 200 m/219 yd on foot from Ctra. Alcúdia | admission free*

FOOD & DRINK

BISTRO MAR ☆

As you enjoy the tasteful fish and meat dishes served in this well-kept bistro you can enjoy the view of the smart yachts and the sea from the patio. *Passeig Marítim 3 | Port d'Alcúdia | tel. 9 71 54 57 04 | www.bistromar.com | closed in winter | Moderate*

CAN PUNYETES

Andalucian watering hole in Port d'Alcúdia, small and always packed, serving a huge choice of the best tapas. *C/ Barques 1 | tel. 9 71 54 83 52 | closed Tue | Budget*

SATYRICÓN

In the lavishly restored former cinema of Alcúdia (note the fabulous ceiling fresco!), you can experience the joys of ancient Roman culinary culture. *Plaça Constitució 4 | tel. 9 71 54 49 97 | daily | Moderate*

few columns and the foundation walls of the *Casa de la Portella. Av. Prínceps d'Espanya | Mon–Fri 9:30am–8:30pm, Sat/Sun 9:30am–2:30pm | admission 3 euros incl. Museu Monogràfic*

MUSEU MONOGRÀFIC DE POLLENTIA

The model of a Roman house is helpful if you want to draw up a picture of what Pollentia used to be like. The museum houses finds from Talaiotic and Roman times, with important archaeological pieces from Pollentia. *C/ Sant Jaume 30 | Mon–Fri 9:30am–8:30pm, Sat/Sun 9:30am–2:30pm | admission see Ciutat de Pollentia*

TOWN WALL

In 1298, under King Jaume II, work started on the town wall as a defence against pirate raids. Up to 1660, several bulwarks and a second ring of walls were added. The parish church of *Sant Jaume (May–Oct Mon–Sat 10am–1pm, for Mass Tue–*

SHOPPING

The Carrer Major features many small shops and boutiques. The shop at number 19 sells fashion accessories and costume jewellery. *Àgata (no. 48)* stocks a wealth of rocks and minerals, and *Oska (no. 34a)* is a fashion boutique. *Sa Cisterna* at the corner of the eponymous side street offers a well-stocked wine bodega *(closed Thu)* alongside a Mallorcan delicatessen.

LEISURE & SPORTS

The bays of Pollença and Alcúdia provide good sailing and windsurfing zones, suitable for beginners too. The sweeping sandy beach of Alcúdia is ideal for children, as it remains shallow far into the sea.

CLUB DE GOLF ALCANADA ⭐

The island's prettiest golf course: 16 of the 18 holes boast sea views; the clubhouse has a good restaurant and panoramic terrace. *Tel. 9 71 54 95 60 | green fee 150 euros*

WIND & FRIENDS WATERSPORTS

Sailing and windsurfing school on the beach at the Hotel Sunwing Alcudia Beach. *Mobile tel. 6 61 74 54 14 | www.windfriends.com | 5-day sailing course 260 euros, 5-day windsurf course 240 euros*

ENTERTAINMENT

The *Auditorio (tel. 9 71 89 71 85)* opposite the town wall hosts theatre performances and concerts from pop to classical. The most popular clubs are *Menta* and *Magic* (near the *Burger King* roundabout).

WHERE TO STAY

BOTEL ALCUDIAMAR CLUB

Unique location at the end of the jetty of Port d'Alcúdia, surrounded by the sea. Exotic outdoor pool, spa area, direct access to the marina. *107 rooms | tel. 9 71 89 72 15 | www.botelalcudiamar.es | Expensive*

⭐ **La Victoria Peninsula**
Pretty towns with villas, romantic coves and a hike to Penja Rotja for dream views → p. 64

⭐ **Capdepera**
A castle out of a picture book. Between the old towers, walls and battlements, it is almost as though you can still hear the battle cries ringing out as pirates attack → p. 69

⭐ **S'Albufera**
Here you can discover Mallorca's primeval landscape on a bike ride through the nature park's wetlands of reeds and orchids and bird habita → p. 71

⭐ **Formentor Peninsula**
Panoramic views and sunset at the foot of Talaia d'Albercutx → p. 74

⭐ **Es Arenal**
Swimming, searching for seashells and taking a stroll without any of the hustle and bustle: the protected dune beach near Son Serra de Marina is still surprisingly tranquil → p. 70

⭐ **Santuari de Lluc**
Mighty ruins, rugged cliffs and the smell of eucalyptus at Mallorca's most important pilgrimage site → p. 75

MARCO POLO HIGHLIGHTS

CAS FERRER NOU

A forge has been turned into a small modern design hotel with six pretty rooms, all styled differently. *C/ Pou Nou 1 | tel. 9 71 89 75 42 | www.nouhotelet.com | Moderate–Expensive*

SON SIURANA 🌐 ☀

In 1999, this 250-year-old family estate was converted into a pretty country hotel with dream views, a pool and seven luxurious holiday apartments. *8 km (5 miles) southwest of town, Ctra. Palma–Alcúdia at km 42.8 | tel. 9 71 54 96 62 | www.sonsiurana.com | Moderate–Expensive*

WHERE TO GO

LA VICTORIA PENINSULA ⭐ ☀
(149 D–E 2–3) (🗺 M–N 2–3)

The road from Alcúdia (well signposted) leads past the pretty villas of *Mal Pas* and *Bonaire*, with marina, to then wind along romantic small bays 6 km (3.7 miles) up to the *Ermita de la Victoria*. The locals revere the *Virgen de la Victoria*, a Gothic figure of the Virgin Mary and patron saint of Alcúdia, which according to legend once saved the town from pirates. Dating from 1679, the church appears like a fortress. Next to the church, the ☀ *Mirador (tel. 9 71 54 71 73 | www.miradordelavictoria. com | closed Mon | Moderate)* with terrace and views of Pollença bay serves day trippers. Along the way to the *Ermita de la Victoria* a perfectly laid-out picnic site has an inviting location by the sea. From the Ermita, the INSIDER TIP hike along the high cliffs up to *Penja Rotja* is well worth doing for the superb views across the bay of Pollença, and only takes about 45 minutes. The path is signposted, but does at one point require a head for heights!

ARTÀ

(155 D2–3) (🗺 P5) This small rural town (pop. 7400) in the farthest northeast is crowned by a forbidding citadel, within which lies the Sant Salvador pilgrimage church.

A bit further down, the terraced village is dominated by the equally fortress-like parish church, of Arabic origin. Cypresses and almond trees dot the ochre of the walls with green. In terms of scenery, expect a few fortified manor houses, flowering gardens and small squares, many bars and a few restaurants. Old traditions, such as raffia and basket weaving, as well as the devil-dancing festivals dedicated to Sant Antoni, are still observed here. The weekly market is held on a Tuesday.

SIGHTSEEING

CASA DE CULTURA DE NA BATLESA

In the "house of culture" the foundation of the painter Miguel Barceló – a genius of the contemporary scene – presents a documented show of his works. *C/ de Ciutat | Mon–Fri 11am–2pm and 6–8pm*

SES PAÏSSES

This Talaiotic settlement is one of the island's best-kept and best-preserved; from 1300 BC to Roman domination in the first century BC it was inhabited by around 300 people. The main entrance and the exterior wall built from extremely heavy megalith blocks will not fail to impress. The centrally positioned *talaia* (watchtower) is said to have been the abode of the chiefs; a good English-language brochure is available. *Past the abandoned railway station right at Ctra. Artà–Capdepera (signposted) | Mon–Fri 10am–5pm, Sat and in winter 10am–2pm | admission 2 euros*

Cypresses line the Way of the Cross leading to San Salvador and up to the fortress

SANT SALVADOR ☆

From the parish church, 180 steps of the Stations of the Cross (*calvario*), lined by cypresses, lead to the fortress. Under King Jaume I the Arabic *almudaina* (fortified palace) was turned into a bulwark of Christianity. Inside the pilgrimage church the painting on the right-hand side illustrates the handing over of Mallorca to the Christian king by the Arab wali. Legends surround the locally revered 17th-century Madonna, telling of how she repeatedly saved the town from pirate attack. Don't forget to take in the view from the surrounding wall of the harmonious semicircle formed by the town. *Daily 10am–6pm*

FOOD & DRINK/ WHERE TO STAY

JARDI D'ARTÀ

Thanks to extensive renovations, the former Hotelito s'Abeurador has been turned into a classy boutique hotel with a restaurant. *13 rooms | C/ Abeurador 21 | tel. 9 71 83 52 30 | www.hotel-arta.com | closed Jan–March | Expensive*

SANT SALVADOR

This stately town house in the upper part of town with swimming pool scores points with its mix of antique and modern interiors – as well as its light Mediterranean dishes served in three in-house restaurants. Occasional live concerts. *8 rooms | C/ Castellet 7 | tel. 9 71 82 95 55 | www.santsalvador.com | Expensive*

SON GENER

Rural 18th-century estate converted into a picture-perfect design finca. *10 rooms | Ctra. Son Servera–Artà at km 3 | tel. 9 71 18 36 12 | www.songener.com | Expensive*

SHOPPING

Artá's pedestrian zone is *Carrer Antoni Blanes*: at number 7 you will find *Georg's*, with his motto: "savour all the joys life has to offer"; an interestingly decorated shop selling local delicatessen products, design for the home as well as art; make sure you try the date vinegar! No. 4 houses the *pedra i flor* shop, a great place to browse for everything you didn't know you needed. *Can Pantalí* at no. 21 is the island's last surviving basket shop selling crafts from Artá and other places.

WHERE TO GO

CALA TORTA/CALA MITJANA
(155 E1) (*Q4*)
A 10-km (6 mile) access road leads to the pretty beaches *Cala Torta* and *Cala Mitjana.* The signposted road starts past Artá on the way to Capdepera; though it doesn't quite reach the beaches, leaving you with a 1-km (0.6 mile) hike at the end.

ERMITA DE BETLEM (155 D2) (*O4*)
To those who brave the serpentine bends leading across the rather barren-looking *Puig de sa Font Crutia*, the gardens and the hermitage will appear like a mirage. The last monks moved to their order's headquarters in the capital Palma in 2010, but you may still visit the chapel of the monastery with its avenue of cypresses, and the ⁜ *mirador* with sweeping views across the bay of Alcúdia. The nearby holy well of *Sa Font* makes an idyllic place for a picnic. *The road begins at Artà Castle (approx. 9.5 km/5.9 miles)*

CALA RAJADA

(155 F2) (*Q5*) **Cala Rajada's idyllic port and its fishermen have managed to** weather the boom in tourism that the largest resort in the northeast has been experiencing since the 1960s.

This town with its beautiful sea promenade has just 6100 inhabitants – and about 15,000 tourist beds. In truth, Cala Rajada, the Bay of Rays, consists of a whole string of rock-lined *calas*. There are many to choose from: broad *Cala Agulla* with its fine sands, the beach of *Son Moll*, small and overrun in the summer, tiny pretty *Cala Gat*, and *Cala de Sa Font* beach, popular with sports lovers. Lined with pines, Cala Agulla is truly beautiful, as is *Cala Mesquida*, 10 km (6 miles) away. The easy, 6 km/3.8 mile INSIDER TIP ▶ hike along the coast *(route 1.2)* from Cala Gat to Cala Agulla leads past the harbour and to the *lighthouse*. On a clear day, you will be able to see all the way to Menorca from here.

SIGHTSEEING

SA TORRE CEGA

Following a devastating storm, the gardens, a paradise covering 60,000 m² above the port, were closed for nine years. In 2010 the sculptures, gardens and the exhibition inside the manor house belonging to the March family were reopened to visitors. *C/ Juan March 2 | guided tours only after registration with Martina: tel. 6 89 02 73 53 | promocio@ajcapdepera.net | Feb–April Wed/Sat 11am–12:30pm, Fri 11am, May–Nov Wed–Fri 10:30am–noon, Sat/Sun 11am–6pm | admission 4.50 euros*

INSIDER TIP seafood restaurants that are supplied daily by the local fishermen, e.g. *Ses Ancores (C/ Leonor Servera 83 | tel. 9 71 56 58 48 | closed Wed lunchtime | Moderate– Expensive)* or *Es Llaüt (C/ Ingeniero Gabriel Roca 2 | tel. 9 71 56 35 61 | www.restauranteesllaut.com | daily | Moderate)*. Ask for the prices; fresh Mallorca fish is expensive!

CAMARONES MOLI VELL

The 200-year-old mill serves delicious seafood, steaks and salads. Large terrace, quiet location. *Ctra. Capdepera–Arta km 1.1 | tel. 9 71 56 48 72 | closed lunchtime and Tue | Moderate*

FOOD & DRINK

Seafood fans flock to Cala Rajada's harbour where you can find great

ENTERTAINMENT

Spreading out around the largest club in Cala Rajada, the centrally located *Bole-*

Cala Gat to the north of Cala Rajada is tiny and terrific

Impressive colours of a world below ground: the stalactite caves of Coves d'Artà

ro, you will find a clutch of cheesy tourist Mallorca bars. Trendsetters enjoy the *Chocolate* open-air bar, the *Physical* club and the *Casa Nova* bar, a local institution with its fair share of VIP visitors.

WHERE TO STAY

FONDA LAS PALMERAS
The basic family hotel is located 4 km / 2.5 mi outside of Cala Rajada in the tourist resort of Font de Sa Cala. The hotel offers German cuisine and friendly service. *32 rooms | C/ Gatova 34 | Bajada Taconera | tel. 9 71 56 34 69 | www.laspalmeras. de | Budget*

SES ROTGES
Small cosy hotel at the harbour, creative cuisine at the *restaurant,* welcoming atmosphere. *20 rooms | C/ Rafael Blanes 21 | tel. 9 71 56 31 08 | www.sesrot ges.com | Moderate*

WHERE TO GO

CANYAMEL (155 F3) (𝄽 Q6)
This small holiday resort 10 km (6 miles) south of Cala Rajada has a sandy beach about 300 m/328 yd wide, with a reed-fringed lagoon. The 18-hole links belonging to the *Canyamel Golf Club (tel. 9 71 84 13 13 | green fee 76–98 euros)* ranks among the more difficult ones. Directly above the beach and a treat for all senses: the hotel *Cap Vermell (11 rooms | tel. 9 71 84 16 27 | www.grupocapvermell. com | Expensive)* with spa and the restaurant *Vintage 1934 (Expensive)*. Boasting a splendid location on 🌊 rocky cliffs, the rural *Can Simoneta* hotel *(18 rooms | tel. 9 71 81 61 10 | www.cansimoneta.com | Expensive)* with minimalist décor has its own access to the sea via a spiral stair. The rustic restaurant *Porxada de Sa Torre (tel. 9 71 84 13 10 | www.porxadadesa torre.es | closed Mon and Dec–Feb | Budg-*

et–Moderate) in a medieval fortified tower on the road to Artà is well-known for its wonderful suckling pig.

CAPDEPERA ★ ⋙ (155 F2) *(𝄞 Q5)*

This town (pop. 11,400) is crowned by a castle *(www.castellcapdepera.com | daily 9am–8pm, in winter until 5pm | admission 3 euros)*, the best-preserved and largest on the island. In the 14th century, the walkable sturdy defensive walls framed Capdepera as it then was, the church, town houses and soldiers' barracks. On a clear day, you can see the neighbouring island of Menorca, only 75 km (47 miles) away. Surrounded by 15 ha/37 acres of untouched countryside, you can see the fortress from the country estate hotel ⋙ *Cases de Son Barbassa (Ctra. Cala Mesquida | Camí de Son Barbassa | Tel. 9 71 56 57 76 | www.sonbarbassa.com | Expensive)*. The rooms and apartments are furnished simply, but beautifully. Wonderfully relaxing: splashing in the outdoor jacuzzi while watching sheep graze. Try out the sophisticated Mediterranean cuisine and good wines in the terrace restaurant even if you are not spending the night at the Cases de Son Barbassa. *8 km (5 miles) from Cala Rajada*

COVES D'ARTÀ CAVES (155 F3) *(𝄞 Q6)*

The soot-blackened maw-like entrance to this imposing cave is located above the sea near Canyamel. *www.cuevasdearta. com | 40-minute guided tours, daily 10am–6pm, in winter until 5pm | admission 14 euros*

CAN PICAFORT

(154 B1) *(𝄞 M–N4)* **In summer, the rather faceless resort Can Picafort (pop.** **7300) with many bars and shops and a 5 km (3 miles) sandy beach becomes fairly lively.**

The eastern beach of *Son Bauló* marks the beginning of a protected section of coast.

SIGHTSEEING

SON REAL

This rural estate houses an interesting museum presenting island life in the 19th and 20th centuries and a history video on the finca. A walk through ancient macchia brings you to the impressive INSIDER TIP *necropolis of Son Real* on the sea. Hundreds of people were buried here between the 7th and 2nd centuries BC. The 300 skeletons and funeral offerings found here are kept in Barcelona. *On the Ma12, km 17.7 | daily 9:30am–1:30pm | admission free | bike rental 5 euros/day*

FOOD & DRINK

MANDILEGO

The finest fish dishes are served here in a nautical ambiance. *C/ Isabel Garau 49 | tel. 9 71 85 00 89 | closed Mon and mid-Dec–mid Feb | Expensive*

ES MOLINO

On simple wooden chairs under pine trees you munch the INSIDER TIP best charcoal-grilled rabbit on the island. *C/ Badía | next to Hotel Sarah | tel. 9 71 85 02 49 | evenings only, closed Mon | Budget*

LEISURE & SPORTS

Accompanied hacks can be booked through *Rancho Grande (Ctra. Artà at km 13.6 | tel. 9 71 85 41 21 | www.ranchograndemallorca.com | 29 euros/hour, hack to the beach 50 euros)*.

WHERE TO STAY

ES BAULÓ PETIT HOTEL
Situated 500 m/546 yd from the beach in the quiet Son Bauló district, this small hotel with apartments and studios makes a pleasant change with its high-class furnishings and good service. *70 rooms | Av. Santa Margalida 28 | tel. 9 71 85 00 63 | www.esbaulo.com | Moderate*

PREDIO SON SERRA
This rustic finca hotel in the backcountry is an idyllic setting perfect for nature lovers and horseback riders. *15 bungalows | Ctra. Muro | tel. 9 71 53 79 80 | www.fincason-serra.com | Expensive*

WHERE TO GO

COLÒNIA DE SANT PERE
(154 C2) (Ø O4)
This sleepy-looking village (pop. 550) on the eastern end of Alcúdia Bay some

LOW BUDGET

An overnight stay in one of the 110 former monks' cells in the *Santuari de Lluc* (see p. 75) *(tel. 9 71 87 15 25)* will only set you back 43 euros (Nov–Jan for two people), including central heating and a bathroom.

On Tuesdays, you can take in the beautiful rose gardens and collection of historic childrens' portraits at the *Fundación Yannick y Ben Jakober (Camino de Ronda 10 | Mal Pas near Alcúdia | www.fundacionjakober.org | Fri–Wed 10am–6pm, Thu 10am–noon)*, which normally cost 10 euros, for free.

20 km (12.5 miles) east of town makes for a good destination for long beach walks from Can Picafort, or the starting point for hikes on the Ferrutx Peninsula. The town has a pretty boulevard along the sea lined by a few bars and restaurants. The pretty restaurant & bar *Sa Xarxa (tel. 971 58 92 51 | www.sa-xarxa.com)* sits on one end.

SON SERRA DE MARINA
(154 B–C2) (Ø N5)
This recent holiday resort (pop. 550) in Wild West decor 8 km (5 miles) southeast of Can Picafort offers beach bars and restaurants with terraces. Behind, the little-frequented protected dune beach of ★ *Es Arenal* stretches for some 2.5 km (1.5 miles) to Colònia de Sant Pere; there are no deckchairs or parasols available however. At the very end nudism is tolerated. A *talaiot* marks the access road at kilometre 14.2 on the road leading to Artà.

MURO

(148 C5) (Ø L4–5) **Heavily agricultural Muro (pop. 6800) is one of the oldest settlements on the island, having received town status as early as 1300.**
Muro's monumental parish church – boasting a former defensive tower, today the belltower, and linked to the church by a bridge – is as impressive as the stately old townhouses in the *Comtat* part of town. At their weekly market on a Sunday, the people of Muro stay mostly amongst themselves.

SIGHTSEEING

MUSEU ETNOLÒGIC DE MURO
The ethnological museum housed in a 17th-century townhouse shows traditional crafts and living quarters, illustrating rural life in the olden days. *C/ Major 15 |*

Sept–July Tue–Sat 10am–3pm, Thu also 5–8pm, Sun 10am–2pm | admission free

FOOD & DRINK

SA FONDA
A large bar and a small dining room, a barbecue, and an open fireplace in the winter provide the simple setting for solid homemade fare. *C/ Sant Jaume 1 | tel. 9 71 53 79 65 | daily | Budget*

WHERE TO STAY

PARC NATURAL
This three-storey complex on the Platja de Muro with its fine sand greets guests with a gigantic entrance: a glass cathedral for sun worshippers with all luxuries. *140 rooms | tel. 9 71 89 20 17 | Expensive*

WHERE TO GO

S'ALBUFERA ★ ●
(148–149 C–D4) *(∅ L–M 3–4)*
Covering 17 km²/6.56 squ. miles, the natural park situated about 5 km (3.1 miles) northeast of Muro is teeming with life, and you can be right in the middle. More than 10,000 migratory birds pass through; there are amphibians, wild horses and orchids. The flat terrain is best explored by bike; bike rental in Port d'Alcúdia or Pollença, e.g. at *Sport Bequi (tel. 9 71 54 56 64 | www.sportbequi. com)* or *New Horizon (tel. 9 71 59 79 87 | www.newhorizon.es)*. Bring your binoculars! Information at the *Centre Recepció* in the park *(tel. 9 71 89 22 50). Ctra. Alcúdia–Can Picafort | entrance at the English bridge | April–Sept 9am–6pm, Oct–March 9am–5pm*

Who's going to argue? In S'Albufera, there is plenty of room for all cattle egrets

comes alive on a Tuesday, market day, when in the *Sa Galerie* bar old and young rub shoulders at the tapas counter. Traditional crafts such as glass blowing, basket weaving and pottery have survived here. Watch glass blowers in action in the *Menestralía* manufacture *(exit 35 of the Palma–Alcúdia motorway)*. Also worth seeing are the bizarre stalactite caves of ● *Coves de Campanet (exit 37 | www.covesdecampanet.com | May–Oct daily 10am–6:30pm, Nov–April 10am–5:30pm | admission 14 euros)*.

CAMPANET ☌ **(153 D–E1)** *(∅ K4)*
This strung-out quiet village (pop. 2600) 8 km (5 miles) northeast of Inca really

SA POBLA (148 B–C4) *(∅ L4)*
While this farming village (pop. 12,700) some 5 km (3.1 miles) outside Muro

POLLENÇA

might not be pretty, it is Mallorca's agricultural heart and has preserved some characteristics that have long died out elsewhere: traditional celebrations such as Sant Antoni and the rural Sunday market, fringed with tapas bars offering spicy regional dishes. On hot August nights, while much of the island holds chillout sessions and beach parties, hundreds of music lovers descend on the market square for the INSIDER TIP *Jazz Festival sa Pobla (jazz.sapobla.cat)* to listen to renowned international bands.

POLLENÇA

(148 B2) (*K–L2*) **The rural town (pop. 16,100) in the far north of the island has an atmosphere all of its own.**
The mostly wealthy Pollençins cultivate their own dialect, traditional crafts, and the arts in general. With a dozen art galleries, as well as the annual international music festival, Pollença definitely stands out from the rest of the provincial towns.

SIGHTSEEING

CALVARI
365 steps along the Stations of the Cross lead to a small pilgrimage church with a great view. *Behind the market square, past the Rooster Fountain (signposted)*

CASA MUSEU DIONÍS BENNÀSSAR
The local painter Dionís Bennàssar (1904–67) belonged to the group around the Art Nouveau painter Hermenegildo Anglada Camarasa. His house is today run as a museum, showing 240 of his works. *C/ Roca 14 | www.museudionisbennassar.com | April–Oct Tue–Sun 10:30am–7pm*

A place with character: view over the market square of Pollença

PORT DE POLLENÇA

Stretching out west from the fishing port and marina of Pollença Bay, the island's most beautiful pedestrian promenade runs under ancient pines and is flanked by pretty villas and hotels from the early 20th century.

PUIG DE MARIA ☆

The best way to access the city's mountain (333 m/1093 ft high), crowned by the former convent of *Mare de Déu del Puig,* is to stop the approach when you reach the last houses. From here start walking, first on the road, then on the ancient pilgrimage path. Your reward will be a stunning view and a pit stop at the convent's cafébar. *Ctra. Palma–Pollença at km 51*

SANTO DOMINGO

In August, the courtyard of the former Dominican monastery (today an old people's home), framed by cloisters, hosts an international music festival *(www.festivalpollenca.com);* on winter Sundays, Mallorcan folklore takes over. The *Museu Municipal* displays finds from Talaiotic times, and a picture gallery is also housed here. *July–Sept Tue–Sat 10am–1pm and 5:30–8:30pm, Aug until midnight, Sun 10am–1pm | admission 1.50 euros*

FOOD & DRINK

ARGOS ☆

Thanks to the plain interior of the restaurant of the hotel La Goleta, nothing distracts you from its creative Mediterranean cuisine – except, perhaps, the ocean view. *Paseo Saralegui 118 | Port de Pollença | tel. 9 71 59 79 87 | www.lagoletahoteldemar. com/argos | daily | Moderate–Expensive*

BELLAVERDE ✪

It is not possible to get any greener than it is in the restaurant of Pension Bellav-

ista: the divine gardens of the Bellaverde provide just the right setting for the creative vegetarian recipes. *C/ de les Monges 14 | Port de Pollença | mobile tel. 6 75 60 25 28 | closed Mon | Moderate*

CELLER LA PARRA

Over-the-top decoration, but **INSIDER TIP** authentic island cuisine. Excellent paella. *Port de Pollença, C/ Joan XXIII 84 | tel. 9 71 86 50 41 | daily | Budget–Moderate*

LA LLONJA ☆

The old fish market has been turned into one of the best gourmet restaurants in the north with a beautiful view of the harbour from upstairs and a sunny bistro below. *Moll Vell | tel. 9 71 86 84 30 | www.restaurantlallonja.com | daily, closed mid-Dec–April | Moderate–Expensive*

SHOPPING

GALERÍA MAIOR

The most avant-garde of the local galleries has an extensive repertoire of international artists. *Plaça Major 4*

SUNDAY MARKET

Sit, watch, shop: On Sunday mornings a lot is going on on the large market square. You can buy fruit and vegetables, ✪ regional products, crafts as well as honey from Artà at the stall Mel de na Marta, surrounded by bars such as the *Can Moixet.*

LEISURE & SPORTS

GOLF POLLENÇA

9-hole golf links, with lovely far-reaching views from the ☆ clubhouse with swimming pool and restaurant. *Ctra. Palma–Pollença | at km 49 | tel. 9 71 53 32 16 | green fee 45 euros*

SAIL & SURF
Mallorca's largest sailing and windsurfing school also offers boat hire. *Passeig Saralegui 134 | tel. 9 71 86 53 46 | www.sailsurf.de/en/*

WHERE TO STAY

BELLAVISTA
The owner of the small inn is warm-hearted and loves animals. Individually decorated rooms, large terrace. Breakfast is served at the Bellaverde restaurant next door. *15 rooms | C/ Monges 14 | Port de Pollença | tel. 9 71 86 46 00 | www.pensionbellavista.com | Moderate*

DESBRULL
Pleasant minimalist B&B hotel at the Santo Domingo monastery. *6 rooms | tel. 9 71 53 50 55 | www.desbrull.com | Moderate*

ILLA D'OR
Traditional establishment with swimming pool and beauty spa at the end of the promenade; a good ☙ terrace restaurant with sea views forms part of the parcel. *120 rooms | tel. 9 71 86 51 00 | www.hotelillador.com. | Moderate–Expensive*

JUMA
Renovated town hotel right on the market square. *7 rooms | tel. 9 71 53 50 02 | www.hoteljuma.com | Moderate*

INSIDER TIP ▸ SON BRULL
This luxurious finca hotel features an unusual, low-key and very modern decor in a 250-year-old building. The excellent in-house gourmet restaurant *365* (named thus for being open all year round) shares the same design, and has an airy terrace. *At the foot of the Puig de Maria, Ctra. Palma–Pollença at km 49.8 | tel. 9 71 53 53 53 | www.sonbrull.com | Expensive*

WHERE TO GO

CALA SANT VICENÇ (148 C1) (*ω L1*)
Small quiet villa resort some 4 km (2.5 miles) northeast of Port de Pollença can easily be reached by bike. Rent it from *Velo-Plus (www.veloplus.info)* in Pollença. The two sandy bays are set against the mountain backdrop of the INSIDER TIP ▸ *Cavall Bernat* whose sheer rock face rises up from the sea. The mountain massif turns different colours depending on the season and the position of the sun. In the afternoons in February and March, the shadow on the rock assumes the shape of a horse and rider: a motif that has inspired countless painters and photographers. The *Cala Sant Vicenç (38 rooms | tel. 9 71 53 02 50 | Expensive)* with garden and well-kept restaurant – a text-book example of hotel renovation – is right in the centre of town. A pine grove with sea views houses the simple family guest house of *Los Pinos (19 rooms | tel. 9 71 53 12 10 | www.hostal-lospinos.com | Budget)* with pool. On the ☙ terrace restaurant *Cala Barques (closed in winter | Moderate)* you can enjoy fabulous sea views with your fresh grilled fish.

FORMENTOR PENINSULA ★ ☙
(149 D–E 1–2) (*ω M–N 1–2*)
The long, narrow peninsula of sheer cliffs sees many visitors. It is worth timing your trip for early morning and late afternoon, when there is a chance of less traffic. This 18-km (11 miles) dream route can easily turn into a nightmare when before the cape the tourist coaches and rental cars can no longer move forwards or backwards. Of more interest than the cape itself is the ☙ *mirador* on the pass with the photogenic rocky islet of *Es Colomer*, the steep 200 m/656 ft-high rock faces and the ● pirate tower *Talaia d'Albercutx*. The ascent takes around half and hour

The church of Lluc convent houses the highly revered statue of the Moreneta

and is rewarded with panoramic views across half the island, and the most spectacular sunset for miles around. The famous sandy beach of *Cala Pi* at the no less famous hotel *Barceló Formentor (108 rooms, 16 suites | Platja de Formentor 3 | tel. 9 71 89 91 00 | www.barceloformentor. com | Expensive)* is pretty but narrow, attracting too many people. More secluded (if only reachable on foot) are the two natural bays of *Cala Figuera* and *Cala Murta*.

SANTUARI DE LLUC ★ (147 F3) (*Ø J3*)

Against an imposing mountain backdrop all around it, amidst fragrant eucalyptus trees and shher rocks, Mallorca's most important pilgrimage site lies 16 km (10 miles) north of Inca in a valley at an altitude of 525 m/1,722 ft. Coachloads of visitors make their way to the *Moreneta*, the Black Madonna in the monastery church.

Picnic areas line the monastic complex dating from the 17th and 18th centuries. Legend has it that in the 14th-century a shepherd boy found the statue of the Virgin Mary and took it to the priest at Escorca three times. Every time, the Madonna returned to the place where she had been found, indicating her choice for the spot where a hermitage should be built. The *blavets,* choir boys dressed in the blue and white colours of the monastic choir school, have been singing at Mass since the 16th century. The cosy mountain restaurant *Es Guix (tel. 9 71 51 70 92 | closed Tue | Moderate)* has a rock pool fed by spring water and good Mallorcan cuisine, about 2 km (1.2 miles) outside Lluc in the direction of Sóller. *Mon–Sat 12:45pm, Sun 11am | 5 euros incl. museum, documentary, garden, pool in the summer, parking*

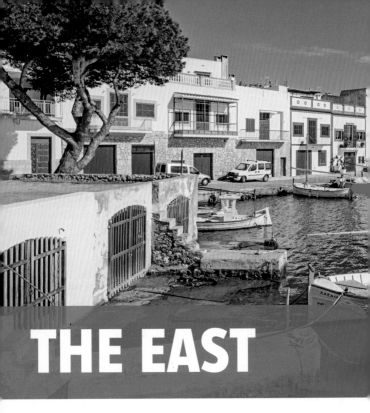

THE EAST

With its white sand, pine-fringed beaches, turquoise sea and white-washed houses, the east coast presents Mallorca's happiest side.

This coast could come close to a Mediterranean idyll, if it wasn't that far too many holidaymakers come here in the high summer months to stay in far too many hotels on the small fjord-like bays, dotted with countless motor yachts and sailboats lying at anchor. Apart from Cala Millor/Sa Coma, parts of the Cales de Mallorca and Portocristo Novo, the holiday zones on the strip of coast between Cap d'es Pins and the Punta de Sa Galera have been constructed in comparatively good taste. Even these however occupy a lot of space and have a disproportionate number of holiday beds for the size of the coves.

One of the island's most beautiful drives, the Ma4014, runs between the coast and the Serra de Llevant mountain range: here almond plantations, gardens with apricot and orange trees, arable fields and vineyards accompany cyclists and drivers on their tour through a gentle landscape of low mountains. The countless beaches along the eastern coast are only accessible by leaving the Ma4014 here and there to take little streets down to the villages on the water. Whilst this takes time, it's well worth it, as the many coves all have their own individual character.

Photo: Port of Portocolom

Mallorca's most charming region: a pretty holiday drive connects caves with picture-perfect ports and beaches

FELANITX

(158–159 C–D2) *(M M–N9)* **At first glance you wouldn't think that the sleepy rural town of Felanitx has 17,300 inhabitants – but on a Sunday the weekly market breathes life into the area around Plaça Espanya. The historic centre is well worth a look on any day.**

In Arab times, Felanitx was at the forefront of *azulejos* (blue tiles) production, paving the way as it were for today's potteries. The former role of Felanitx as a centre of agriculture is still evident, as a few mill towers remain from what used to be a total of 25. Today, the town lives from tourists visiting the nearby coastal resorts, as well as from cultivating wine and fruit, farming cattle and fish, and various small businesses. In 1957 Felanitx saw the birth of Miquel Barceló, arguably the most important Mallorcan contemporary painter. Barceló's works mostly represent nature; two of them are in fact already on show at the Prado in Madrid.

SIGHTSEEING

CALVARI ☀
Atop the Calavari with its simple 19th-century chapel (usually closed), the view of the town is quite spectacular. Starting

FOOD & DRINK/ WHERE TO STAY

EL CASTILLO DEL BOSQUE
The castle-like decor may be a matter of taste, but the Mediterranean menu featuring Mallorcan dishes is entirely recommendable and a favourite among Spanish visitors from the mainland. *On the road to*

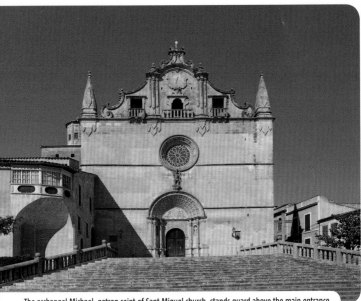

The archangel Michael, patron saint of Sant Miquel church, stands guard above the main entrance

from the church, turn down Carrer Major and then right onto Carrer d'es Call to get to the steps marking the beginning of the Way of the Cross.

SANT MIQUEL PARISH CHURCH
Rising above an imposing flight of steps, the 18th-century church boasts a magnificent rose window and an ornately decorated portal. *Sundays at market times and for Mass*

Portocolom, km 8, large parking lot, but often a lot of traffic | tel. 9 71 82 41 44 | www. elcastillodelbosque.es | Thu–Tue 1–4pm and 7–10:30pm | Moderate

ESTRAGON
Inexpensive, but good: this small terrace restaurant right in the heart of Felanitx town scores with a good-value and tasty daily set menu for 12 euros. À la carte, you can order monkfish, duck or rabbit, for example. *Plaça Perelada 14 | tel.*

9 71 58 33 03 | www.estragon-felanitx.
com | Wed–Sun 1–3pm and 7:30–11pm |
Budget–Moderate

ES PICOT AGROTURISME
Friendly bed & breakfast hotel in the
countryside (at the hamlet of Son Ma-
cia 11 km (6.8 miles) away) with only
five rooms. *Camí de sa Mola, km 3.6 | tel.
6 37 73 79 43 | www.espicot.com | Mod-
erate*

SA POSADA D'AUMALLÍA
The Gomila family has lovingly fur-
nished the 14 rooms in rustic antique
style. *Camino Son Prohens 1027 | tel.
9 71 58 26 57 | www.aumallia.com | Mod-
erate–Expensive*

SON MENUT
Country hotel with stud, pool and restau-
rant. *8 rooms | Camí de Son Negre | ac-
cess from Ma5120 at km 7.5 | tel. 9 71 58
29 20 | www.sonmenut.com | Moderate*

SHOPPING
You shouldn't return home from Felanitx without some sort of earthenware
souvenir. These can be found at, for example, *Cerámiques Mallorca (C/ de Sant
Agustí 50)* or *Call Vermell (C/ Major 44),* a
pottery with an attached shop. .

CANDELA HOME
The objects that gave the shop its name
are sold here of course: candles of all descriptions. A great mix of deco shop, gallery and café. *C/ Major 60*

SUNDAY MARKET
From around 10am the heart of the town
gets busy with open-air and covered markets. There is hardly standing space in the
pubs along the palm-lined *Plaça Espanya.*

WHERE TO GO

CALA MARÇAL (159 E3) *(ᛗ O10)*
This is a sandy bay with little in the way of
greenery, dominated by the hotel of the
same name, 10 km (6 miles) southeast of
town at Portocolom. Behind Cala Marçal
and only accessible on foot, there's the
small, romantic ★ *Cala Brafi,* a beach
that escaped the construction boom. The
way to the bay is a hidden narrow path
running along a wall from the upper part
of town behind Cala Marçal.

CALA SA NAU (159 E4) *(ᛗ O10)*
The relaxed bar *Xiringuito Cala Sa Nau
(mobile tel. 6 37 83 32 76 | www.calasa
nau.com | daily | Moderate)* serves de-
licious hamburgers, the water is turquoise, there are restrooms and sun-
shades and a car park directly adjacent:
the Cala Sa Nau, 12 km/7.5 miles southeast, is the perfect cove for a perfect day.

MARCO POLO HIGHLIGHTS

★ **Cala Brafi**
Enjoy a swim in a romantic
cove with no buildings around
→ p. 79

★ **Portocolom**
This tranquil fishing port with
its colourful boathouses hasn't
yet been discovered by tourists
→ p. 80

★ **Puig de Sant Salvador**
A huge stone cross, a giant figure of Christ and a gorgeous
view → p. 81

★ **Coves del Drac**
This underground lake in the stalactite caves serves as a stage for
music shows → p. 83

CAS CONCOS (158 C3) ( M10)

The drive through fields and hills to this village with 420 inhabitants is part of the attraction. The village itself would not be remarkable if Cas Concos and the surrounding area didn't offer some fine places to visit. Alongside many self-catering fincas scattered throughout the area, there is also a good finca hotel in the shape of the *Sa Galera* estate (*20 rooms | Ctra. Santanyí–Cas Concos at km 6.3 | tel. 9 71 84 20 79 | www.hotels agalera.com | Expensive*). The 13th-century manor house has an attached restaurant. The highly praised, hip *Viena (C/ Metge Obrador 13 | tel. 9 71 84 22 90 | Wed–Mon from 6pm | Moderate)* has lost its founder; the restaurant however carries on with the same menu. A few houses further on (number 23), a Chilean family runs the soberly modern *Can Pelat (tel. 97 13 96 43 | closed lunchtime | Moderate)*, offering imaginative Mediterranean cuisine with a touch of Asia.

CASTELL DE SANTUERI (159 D3) (*N10*)

The ruins of this massive medieval fortification lie on a mountain 7 km (4.3 miles) south of town. It is worth for sweeping views and the place's bizarre feeling of being away from everything. The view ranges far across the countryside and the sea. The website has information on he history of the site. *www.santueri.org | daily 10am–6:30pm, in the winter Sat/Sun 10am–2pm, 4pm–6pm | admission 4 euros*

PORTOCOLOM ★ (159 E3) (*O10*)

The former port of Felanitx, 10 km (6 miles) southeast with its well-preserved fishermen's houses and boathouses, as well as many traditional *llaüts* (Mallorcan fishing boats), has managed to stay as pretty as a picture, but unfortunately it is set to be enlargened. Only *Cala Marçal* has gained modest tourist infrastructure. The largest hotel in town with 347 rooms is the friendly *Club Cala Marsal (tel.*

The rural landscape around Cas Concos at the edge of the Serra de Llevant is idyllic

9 71 82 52 25 | www.hotelclubcalamarsal. com | *Budget–Moderate*). Otherwise, a few small *hostals* offer accommodation. They have been joined along the pretty harbour promenade by *Hostal HPC (14 rooms | C/ Cristófol Colom 5 | tel. 9 71 82 53 23 | www. hostalportocolom.com | Moderate)* . Once a week, its light-filled ☼ restaurant with terrace and harbour views hosts a DJ for entertainment. Next door, *Colón (C/ Cristófol Colom 7 | tel. 9 71 82 47 83 | www. restaurante-colon.com | closed Wed | Expensive)* serves excellent Mediterranean cuisine with a local touch, prepared by well-known Austrian chef Dieter Sögner, in a refined atmosphere. The number of inhabitants (3500) triples in high season, when the residents of Felanitx move into their summer houses. Historical research may say otherwise, but a persistent rumour circulates here whereby Christopher Columbus was born in Portocolom, lending the place its name.

PUIG DE SANT SALVADOR ★ ☼
(159 D3) *(ℳ N9)*

The holy mountain of Felanitx (509 m/1670 ft) is a double summit. The higher peak of the two is crowned by an abandoned monastery with origins in the 13th century. The complex shelters a statue of the Virgin Mary from the same period and a Gothic alabaster altarpiece. An oversized stone cross on the second peak and a huge statue of Christ demonstrate the power of the Church. This unusual place was chosen for the *Petit Hotel Sant Salvador (tel. 9 71 51 52 60 | www.santsalvadorhotel.com | Budget–Moderate)* with 20 rooms, two apartments and a restaurant; a pleasant touch of the modern within historic walls. Tip: look out for specials! You can also stay at the fairly simple monastery, complete with spectacular views all the way across to the Cabrera archipelago. *6 km (3.7 miles) to the southeast*

MANACOR

(154 B–C5) *(ℳ N7)* The island's third-largest municipality (pop. 40,300) gets a fairly bad press in most travel guides. However, the church square with its cafés and bars has kept an authentic feel. More than elsewhere the centre belongs to its inhabitants. Manacor makes a fair living from the souvenir and furniture industry that has settled around the town, and from tourism.

SIGHTSEEING

RAFA NADAL SPORTS CENTRE

Rafa Nadal loves his island and his hometown of Manacor. One could say that he has raised a monument to himself here with his sports centre. The premises of the tennis academy include sports facilities, a hotel for students and a merchandising store. Trophies and prize cups of the tennis star are exhibited in the mu-

LOW BUDGET

The basic *Café d'es Mercat (C/ Major | Felanitx | tel. 9 71 58 00 08 | closed Sat)* opposite the covered market is popular not only at market time on Sunday. The reason? Have a look at the cafe's excellent and good-value daily set menus.

Undiluted rural life: walk or bike the dirt roads to explore the countryside around Felanitx. The town hall has published a pamphlet with possible tours in English that is available free of charge at *www.visitfelanitx. es/en/walks*.

seum *Sport-Xperience (daily 10:15am–5:15pm | admission 12 euros, incl. basement 22 euros). www.rnsportscentre.com*

TORRE DELS ENAGISTES

This fortified tower with palace dates back to the 13th century. Today, it houses the *Historical Museum (summer Mon, Wed–Sat 9:30am–2pm, 6pm–8:30pm, winter Mon–Sat 10am–2pm, 5pm–7:30pm, Sun 10am–1pm | admission free)*, with mosaics and finds from the early Christian basilicas of Son Peretó and Sa Carrotxa at Manacor. The sturdy building alone is worth the visit. *Ctra. Cales de Mallorca, km 1.5*

FOOD & DRINK/ WHERE TO STAY

CAN MARCH

Enjoy modern Mallorcan cuisine in a cosy and somewhat hidden family-run restaurant. *C/ Valéncia 7 | tel. 9 71 55 00 02 | www.canmarch.com | closed Tue–Thu and Sun evenings, closed Mon | Budget–Moderate*

LA RESERVA ROTANA

Luxury finca hotel 4 km (2.5 miles) north of Manacor with its own golf links and a high-end restaurant. *21 rooms, 1 holiday cottage | Camí de S'Avall | at km 3 | tel. 9 71 84 56 85 | www.reservarotana.com | Expensive*

SA PICADA

The tapas and set menus are simple, honest and good. *C/ Alejandro Rosselló 7 | mobile tel. 6 36 86 63 18 | closed Sun | Budget*

SON AMOIXA VELL

Country hotel in a 20-hectare estate with pool and tennis courts, ten rooms, four suites and one apartment. The breakfast buffet for sleepyheads stays open until 11:30am. *Ctra. Cales de Mallorca–Manacor | at km 3.4 | tel. 9 71 84 62 92 | www.sonamoixa.com | Expensive*

SON JOSEP DE BAIX

Six apartments for self-catering nature lovers in a simple but classy farm with pool and its own tiny cove at the end of the world. *Ctra. Portocristo–Portocolom | at km 8.4 | mobile tel. 6 36 41 09 79 | www.sonjosepdebaix.com | Moderate–Expensive*

SHOPPING

INSIDER TIP CAN GARANYA 40

Even if you currently don't need a bird cage or tin plate funnel, you simply must take a look around this general store! It is crammed full of everyday rural items, very few of which are made out of plastic and most of which are made on the island. You will definitely not leave here without some kind of souvenir. A few houses further down, the family runs the shoe store *Can Garanya 51,* where you can find the trendy leather mules called *aubarcas* and hand-sewn espadrilles. *C/ Joan Lliteras 40 | www.cangaranya.com*

WHERE TO GO

CALES DE MALLORCA (159 E2) (*Ø O9*)

18 km (11 miles) southeast of Manacor, this hotel complex of over 7500 beds forms a town of its own really. Continually extended since the 1960s, the place lies above several small and beautiful sandy bays, which in high season can become packed. Also, if you are staying in one of the hotels at the back, it's a fair way to the beaches. A pretty shore promenade and green areas make up for the lack of a centre.

The "Caves of the Dragon" hide away in the rocks on the coast near Porto Cristo

INSIDER TIP ▶ COVA DES COLOMS
(155 D6) (*O8*)

The "cave of pigeons" with its sweet-water lake and bizarre dripstone formations is as large as a cathedral. It can be found below a small headland between the coves of Cala Falcó and Cala Varques and is most easily approached by way of the ocean. The diving schools *Skualo (Tel. 9 71 81 50 94 | www.skualo.com)* in Porto Cristo and Portocolom will take you on board for a half-day excursion *(65 euros).* You can leave your wetsuit and flashlight at home, they are supplied by the tour operator. Cova des Coloms is easy to access, you don't need to be able to dive or climb.

PORTO CRISTO (155 D6) (*P8*)

This town (pop. 7350) 13 km (8 miles) east of Manacor is a pretty place, thanks to its rounded harbour bay and the *torrent,* with *llaüts* and yachts bobbing on it. Portocristo owes its fame to the largest stalactite caves on the island. The

Coves del Hams (www.cuevas-hams.com | daily in summer 10am–5pm, in winter 10am–4pm | admission with digital show 21 euros) are right at the entrance to the town along the road from Manacor. They attempt to emulate the larger neighbouring "Caves of the Dragon" by means of a guided tour, a show on the small underground lake and a virtual Jules Verne show. The ★ *Coves del Drac (Ctra. Cuevas | www.cuevas-deldrach.com | in summer 10am–5pm every hour on the hour except at 1pm, in winter 10:45am, noon, 2pm and 3:30pm | admission 15 euros)* offer no guided tour – leaving everything to the imagination. Here, however, the largest underground lake in the world is the stage for a kitschy but beautiful tourist spectacle: a boat with mini orchestra glides over the lake, which is completely dark at first, then gradually illuminated. Afterwards visitors can go for a short ride on the boat. As the caves attract crowds, it's a good idea to come early in the morning. Access is through the village of Porto Cristo, then follow the brown sign to the southern end of town. The *THB Felip* hotel *(96 rooms | tel. 9 71 82 07 50 | www.thbho tels.com | Moderate)* is situated right on the harbour promenade. The only quiet rooms are at the back. A culinary delight in Porto Cristo hides in a seemingly unspectacular place from the outside bearing the name *Roland (C/ Sant Jordi 5 | tel. 9 71 82 01 29 | www.roland-restaurant.es | daily | Moderate)*. Top-notch international cuisine and good service.

SANT LLORENÇ/ SON SERVERA

(154–155 C–D4) *(Ø O–P 6–7)* **The two communities Sant Llorenç (pop. 8300) and Son Servera (pop. 11,600), situated between Artà and Manacor in the Serra de Llevant, share the coast between Cap d'es Pinar and Punta de Sa Roca.**
The villages are connected by a very scenic road (Ma4030); most inhabitants are involved in the tourism business along the coast. In summer the unfinished neo-Gothic church of Son Servera houses folklore events.

SIGHTSEEING

SA PLETA FREDA
The two tireless proprietors of the gallery located directly next to the church in Son Servera have been exhibiting exciting art for the past 40 years. Its tower-like construction alone makes the gallery worth a visit. *C/ Pleta Freda 2 | Tue–Sat 6:30pm–8:30pm*

FOOD & DRINK/ WHERE TO STAY

PETIT HOTEL CASES DE PULA
Country hotel with ten rooms and suites, as well as a spa, right on the 18-hole Pula Golf course (green fee 78 euros). *6 km (3.7 miles) outside Son Servera on the country road to Capdepera | tel. 9 71 56 74 92 | www.pulagolf.com | Expensive*

WHERE TO GO

CALA BONA/CALA MILLOR
(155 E4–5) *(Ø P6–7)*
Merged together now, the two resorts *Cala Bona* and *Cala Millor* (pop 6600) 4 km (2.5 miles) southeast of Son Servera are connected by a beach about 3 km (1.9 mile) long, boasting fine sand and a pretty promenade for pedestrians only. However it is completely built up. The mainly three- or four-star high-rise hotels with 18,000 beds are in the hands of German

tour operators. The valiant and extremely good-value exception is the *Cala Millor* guesthouse *(C/ Juan Servera Camps 23 (tel. 9 71 58 63 98 | Budget)* with ten rooms, clean and bright. A thoroughly organised bathing operation plus sports and leisure facilities make the double bay child- and family-friendly. Numerous bars and discos such as *Palace Q, Karussell* and *Bananas* ensure that the place stays attractive for young people too. The many cafeterias, such as *Bei Petra (Budget)* right on the beach promenade, have adapted to German guests. A laudable alternative is INSIDER TIP *Can Pistoleta (Na Llambies 23 | daily | Moderate)*, which puts on a huge and very satisfying buffet.

SA COMA (155 E5) (*ψ P7*)

Separated from Cala Millor by the natural rocky outcrop of Punta de n'Amer is the spectacularly white sandy beach of Sa Coma, about 1 km (0.6 mile) long, with a pedestrianised promenade. The backcountry is built up to the hilt with huge hotel complexes. Since his move from Sant Llorenç into the *Protur Hotel Sa Coma Playa (C/ Liles | www.proturhotels.com)*, Michelin-starred chef Tomeu Caldenty continues to spoil his guests in *Es Molí d'en Bou (tel. 9 71 56 96 63 | www.esmolidenbou.es | Expensive)* with excellent Mediterranean dishes. Take note of the specialities of the season!

SA COSTA DES PINS
(155 E–F4) (*ψ Q6*)

The well-heeled pine-fringed villa quarter 5 km (3.1 miles) northeast of Son Servera possesses accommodation to match in the shape of the *Eurotel Golf Punta Rotja (200 rooms | tel. 9 71 81 65 00 | www.eurotelmallorca.com | Expensive)* with its gourmet restaurant and facilities for wellness and thalassotherapy treatments. The sandy beach a bit further south, *Platja d'es Ribell*, has hardly any buildings.

What can they be looking at from the mole of Cala Bona?

THE SOUTH

A flat, dry expanse, this is what the south of Mallorca is like – oh, and hot... The country towns of Llucmajor and Campos divide up the plain amongst themselves, whilst the municipality of Santanyí in the southeast forms part of the gentle foothills of the Serra de Llevant.

Blessed with magnificent white sand dunes and a turquoise sea, the beautiful beaches of S'Estanyol, Sa Ràpita and Colònia de Sant Jordi are almost like the Caribbean.

CAMPOS

(158 A–B3) (₥ K–L 9–10) **With its cattle and dairy farming, Campos is one of the agricultural centres of the island.**

Normally, its straight-as-a-die streets give Campos a rather sleepy air, but on market days, Thursdays and Saturdays, things become livelier.

Campos is said to have existed in Roman times already. The street leading to the municipal salt stocks and the beaches along the south coast are flanked by fields where *alfalfa* (lucerne) and *tàperes* (capers) are cultivated.

SIGHTSEEING

SANT JULIÀ

The star attraction in the parish church is the painting "Santo Cristo de la Paciencia" by Bartolomé Murillo (1618–82); the key to the church is kept at the *rectoría* opposite.

White salt works, green pines, turquoise sea: the beaches and coves where the island is hottest have a Caribbean feel

FOOD & DRINK

MOLI DE VENT

Fans of mills will be captivated by this pretty, perfectly restored restaurant in a mill dating back to 1873 with a garden terrace. The couple who run the place offer Fresh, seasonal cuisine with 4 and 5 course menus (from 40 euros). *C/ Nord 34 | tel. 9 71 16 04 41 | www.moli-de-vent.com. | Thu–Tue 7pm–midnight | Expensive*

SA CANOVA

Traditional seasonal cuisine with exquisite ingredients. The fish comes from the waters of the Cabrera national park, the fruits and vegetables grow right in the garden. *Ronda Estació 36 | tel. 9 71 65 02 10 | Tue–Sat 1:15–3:45pm and 8:15–10:45pm, Sun lunchtime only | Moderate*

SHOPPING

The village shows itself from its most charming side every Saturday morning,

South Sea feeling on Mallorca's most beautiful dune beach : Es Trenc

when anyone who has something to sell gathers on the market square: farmers, artisans, dealers in second-hand goods.

POMAR

This bakery has been a point of reference on the island since 1902; the most popular items purchased here are the *ensaïmadas, cocas* and the home-made chocolates. *Ctra. Major 20–22 | near the church*

WHERE TO STAY

FINCA ES FIGUERAL

This stately farmhouse with swimming pool and many farm animals offers eight rooms and suites as well as an apartment sleeping four people. The ✪ kitchen uses produce from the farm; you can also request **INSIDER TIP** completely vegetarian dishes. *Ctra. Campo–Santanyi | at km 42 | tel. 9 71 65 16 41 | www. esfigueral.com | closed mid-Dec–mid-Feb | Moderate–Expensive*

FINCA SANT BLAI

The four rustic living units of this authentic and cosy country house won't break the bank. If the swimming pool is not enough, visit the beaches of Colónia de Sant Jordi, some 8 km (5 miles) away. *2 km (1.2 miles) outside Campos | tel. 9 71 65 05 67 | www.santblai.com | Moderate*

ES REVELLAR

Relaxation plus country art equals Es Revellar! Located south of Campos, the art hotel with only 14 rooms is more than a holiday dwelling. You will be enchanted by the sculpture park with its fountains and lights. Tours through the park are held Wednesdays and Saturdays and are also open to visitors who are not spending the night at the hotel. *Camí des Revellar, km 3.7 | tel. 9 71 16 02 74 | www.rev ellarartresort.com | Moderate*

WHERE TO GO

BALNEARIO SAN JUAN DE LA FONT SANTA (158 B5) (⌘ L11)

Mallorca's only hot spring has found a fitting setting in the spa hotel *Font Santa (Ctra. Campos–Colónia de Sant Jordi | km 8.2 | tel. 9 71 65 50 16 | www.fontsantahotel.com | Expensive)*. It offers medicinal treatments all your round, a spa and a restaurant that uses market-fresh ingredients. Non-hotel guests pay 85 euros for a day at the spa including lunch.

ES TRENC/PLATJA DE SA RÀPITA ★
(158 A4–5) (*₥ K11*)

Sample some South Sea feeling on Mallorca, 11 km (6.8 miles) south of Campos. Unspoilt by buildings, the two natural beaches *Es Trenc* and *Platja de sa Ràpita* join seamlessly, making them ideal for extended beach walks. About 5 km (3.1 miles) long, Es Trenc is considered Mallorca's most beautiful dune beach – which also means of course that in high summer it can be chock-a-block which also makes the pay car parks *(daily 9am–9pm | day ticket 6 euros, afternoon ticket 4 euros)* pretty full. Park at the yacht harbour of Sa Ràpita to be sure to get your day at the beach off to a relaxed start. You can take the free bus from there to Es Trenc, which leaves every 15 minutes between 10 am and 8.45 pm. Speaking of relaxed: the young proprietors of the restaurant INSIDER TIP *S'Oratge (C/ Llevant 56 | Sa Ràpita | tel. 9 71 64 05 89 | www.soratge.net | March–Oct Tue–Sun, Nov Sat/Sun | Budget)* offer light cuisine with grilled vegetables, fish and meat, all served in a casual atmosphere. An affordable set menu is available at lunchtime, in the evenings the menu includes creative *Pa-amb-oli* variations and cocktails.

LLUCMAJOR

(157 E4) (*₥ J9*) **Llucmajor (pop. 34,600) has made island history as the place where in 1349 the last Mallorcan king, Jaume III, was killed by the troops of his cousin Pedro IV of Aragon, sealing the fate of the independent kingdom of Mallorca.**

A monument on *Plaça Espanya* commemorates these events. A second monument nearby *(Carrer Bisbe Taxaqet)* praises the town's most important craft: shoemaking. On Wednesdays, Fridays and Sundays the vegetable market on the pretty pedestrianised main square shows what else keeps the inhabitants of Llucmajor busy. If you arrive by car, park as early as you can along the main road and walk the rest of the way.

FOOD & DRINK

CAFÈ ARÀBIC

Since 1994, tapas, sandwiches *(llonguets)* and simple Mallorcan dishes have been served here, a café hidden away in a corner of the large town square. You can sit at a comfortable table inside or on the terrace. *C/ Constitució 2 |*

MARCO POLO HIGHLIGHTS

★ **Es Trenc/Platja de sa Ràpita**
Dream beaches as far as the eye can see → p. 89

★ **Capocorb Vell**
Impressive remnants of life 3500 years ago → p. 90

★ **Cala Figuera**
Experience a romantic fishing port like nowhere else on the island → p. 92

★ **Parc Natural Mondragó**
Emerald-green swimming coves with protected backcountry → p. 93

★ **Cabrera**
The boat trip to the protected archipelago lasts about two hours → p. 95

tel. 9 71 12 10 01 | www.cafearabic.es | closed Mon evening and Sun | *Budget*

SHOPPING

ESPART SPORT
Wonderful general stores crammed full of goods like this one are hard to find on the island. The store sells essential and beautiful items at real village prices; most are made in Spain. *C/ d'es Born 17 | Mon–Fri 9:30am–1pm, Sat 9am–1pm*

EDELWEISS
Outdoor gear for climbing enthusiasts? Traditional Alpine dress? No, you will find novel creations by international fashion labels in this well-stocked boutique, which despite its German name is run by Spaniards. *Plaça Espanya 39*

WHERE TO STAY

SON GALILEU
Rustic finca sleeping two to six people and situated on a large estate, with pool and its own farm. 🌐 Breakfast and dinner with produce from the farm on request. *6 km (3.7 miles) south of Llucmajor | tel. 9 71 18 00 29 | www.finca-sllucmajor.com | Budget–Expensive*

SON GUARDIOLA
This finca with swimming pool and Mallorcan cuisine has a relaxed atmosphere; there are eight rooms and three apartments, each with its own entrance. Mallorcan cuisine. *Ctra. Llucmajor–s'Estanyol | km 2.3 | tel. 9 71 12 12 07 | www.songuardiola.com | Moderate*

WHERE TO GO

CAPOCORB VELL ⭐ (157 D6) *(𝄞 H10)*
Arguably Mallorca's best-preserved Talaiotic settlement dates back to around 1400 BC. Prepare to be impressed by the ruined *talaiot* stretching across several levels and the wealth of preserved foundation walls of this residential and defensive complex built from huge stone blocks. *12 km (7.5 miles) south | www.talaiotscapocorbvell.com | Fri–Wed 9am–3pm | admission 2 euros*

INSIDER TIP ▶ SON MUT NOU
(157 D4) *(𝄞 H9)*
What, you are not interested in figs? That will change after a visit to the fig finca. A Mallorcan pharmacist is living out his passion here. He has planted around 1700 trees – more than 800 varieties from 60 countries. Take a tour to find out just why these are so fascinating; in the late summer you can also sample the sweet fruit as part of the tour. You should also try the fig products. *9 km southwest, Ma-19, exit 18, near the Marriot Hotel | Camí d'es Palmer | mobile tel. 6 46 63 32 59 | www.sonmutnou.com | Tue/Thu/Sat 8am–2pm | admission free, group tour 4 euros per person after registration*

SANTANYÍ

(158 C4–5) *(𝄞 M11)* **Quite lively and very popular with Germans is the small, tranquil town of Santanyí (pop. 11,600) whose area includes divine sandy beaches.**

The homogeneous ensemble with its ochre sandstone houses, pedestrianised zone, and many shops, bars and restaurants makes for a rewarding stroll, particularly on market days *(Wed and Sat)*.

SIGHTSEEING

SANT ANDREU
The large village church has one of the best-preserved Baroque organs in Eu-

rope; with 25 pipes per key it is also the largest in Spain. It is in excellent condition, which you can come hear for yourself: between May and September the organ is played during the *Festival Internacional de Música (www.festivalmusicasantanyi.com)*.

ES COC

Traditional Mallorcan dishes with a new twist, served with a smile and at fair prices in a pretty town house. Daily set menu 15 and 25 euros. *C/ Aljub 37 | tel. 9 71 64 16 31 | www.restauranteescoc. com | closed Sun | Moderate*

Mmm, very tasty! More than 800 varieties of these can be found on the fig farm Son Mut Nou

FOOD & DRINK

ANOA

Meals are cooked fresh every day using regional ingredients. Be sure to try the fish soup. *C/ de s'Aljub 32 | tel. 9 71 65 33 15 | www.anoa-santanyi.com | closed Mon, at lunchtime and Nov– March | Moderate–Expensive*

INSIDER TIP ▶ SA BOTIGA

Café serving breakfast and lunch amidst playful Mediterranean decor. *Next to the church | www.sabotiga-santanyi.com | daily | Budget*

PURA VIDA

The southern end of the fishing village of Cala Figuera is home to the Pura Vida. The restaurant, bistro and bar are situated over two floors with a fantastic sea view. It hosts a INSIDER TIP ▶ full moon party every 28 days in summer. Live music takes to the stage in the bistro on Thursdays. Reservations recommended! *C/ Tomarinar 25 | tel. 9 71 16 55 71 | www.pura-vida-mallorca.com | breakfast 10am– 1pm, à la carte 1–10pm | Moderate–Expensive*

Almost too idyllic to be true:
the harbour of Cala Figuera

SHOPPING

ECOTECA/L'ARÇ NATURA 🌱

A growing number of Mallorcans, especially those living in the interior of the island, want to buy naturally produced products. Two organic grocery stores reflect this change. In addition to fresh products from the island, *L'Arç Natura (C/ Bernat Vidal Tomàs 23)* also offers dietary supplements, while the *Ecoteca (C/ Centre 6)* sells natural cosmetics and novel gifts.

TRACES

Come here for unusual and affordable fashions and accessories created by Italian, French and Spanish labels. *C/ Sebastià Vila 11*

WEEKLY MARKET

Stroll through the weekly market featuring numerous Mallorcan products in the pedestrian zone near the town church *(Wed and Sat)*. The surrounding boutiques are also open on market days.

WHERE TO STAY

SON LLORENÇ

Small hotel in the heart of the village of s'Alquería Blanca with eight comfortable rooms named after Mallorca's winds. Breakfast in the dining room or in the patio. *C/ Ramon Llull 7 | tel. 9 71 16 11 61 | www. hotelsonllorenc.com | Moderate–Expensive*

HOTEL SANTANYÍ

This small new town hotel with seven rooms is housed in 300-year-old walls; there is a patio and restaurant too. *Next to the church | tel. 9 71 64 22 14 | www.ho tel-santanyi.com | Expensive*

WHERE TO GO

INSIDER TIP CALA DE SA COMUNA/ CALA S'AMUNIA (158 C5) *(𝟙 M11–12)*

A footpath (about 20 minutes) connects the two natural bays *Cala de Sa Comuna* and *Cala S'Amunia.* Devoid of any infrastructure, these represent arguably the last beach paradise on Mallorca's eastern coast that is accessible by land. Access to Cala S'Amunia is by a set of steep steps down to the sea (in a bend in the village, to the left of a private house). *9 km (5.6 miles) south of Santanyí*

CALA FIGUERA ⭐ (159 D5) *(𝟙 N11)*

About 5 km (3.1 miles) southeast of Santanyi, this resort might not have a beach, but instead it is the most idyllic fishing port on the island. On weekdays between 3 and 5pm in particular, the time when the INSIDER TIP fishing boats return to port, visitors can catch an impressive glimpse of the world of the fishermen. A very good-value and clean accommodation option is the little⊙ Mar Blau hostal (20 rooms | tel. 9 71 64 52 27 | www.mar blau.eu | Moderate) near the port with a small attached apartment complex, Vista al Mar (Budget). The Spanish hotel owners' effort to do their bit for sustainable green tourism can be seen in many small details. The ⬩⬩ Bon-Bar sits directly above the harbour with views of the ships sailing in and out of the harbour, while ⬩⬩ L'Arcada in the pedestrian zone (but still with sea views) serves fresh fish tapas.

CALA D'OR/PORTOPETRO
(159 D–E4) (ⓜ N11)

Built in the Ibizan style with whitewashed houses framed by climbing flowers, these two holiday resorts 7 km (4.4 miles) east of Santanyi have nearly merged together now. While Cala d'Or has a perfect tourist infrastructure, the harbour village of Portopetro has preserved a bit of its laid-back character. Cala d'Or has half a dozen small beaches. In terms of hotels, Inturotel Cala Esmeralda (151 rooms | tel. 9 71 65 71 11 | Moderate) right on the bay of the same name has a genteel style, adults only; Sensimar Rocador (210 rooms | tel. 9 71 65 77 25 | www.nordotel.com/es/ho tel-rocador-cala-dor-mallorca-baleares. html | Budget) lies above Cala Gran. An exemplary green hotel that uses solar energy, has its own recycling facilities and maintains low water usage levels is the prettily situated ⊙ Robinson Club Cala Serena (280 rooms | www.robinson-ep. com | closed Nov–mid March | Moderate–Expensive). On the harbour, the fairly basic Cafetería La Caracola (tel. 9 71 65 70 13 | daily | Budget) serves no-frills regional cuisine. Top-of-the-catch fish and a sumptuous tasting menu with harbour views for 60 euros can be had at ⬩⬩ Port Petit (tel.

9 71 64 30 39 | www.portpetit.com | June–Sept closed Tue lunchtime | Expensive).

CALA SANTANYÍ (159 D5) (ⓜ M11)

Blessed with white sands this pretty bay, situated about 3.5 km (2.2 miles) south of Santanyí, is fringed by some hotels and summer houses. The renovated hotel Cala Santanyí (tel. 9 71 16 55 05 | www. hotelcalasantanyi.com | closed Nov–Easter | Moderate) directly on the bay has 24 rooms and 28 apartments. Clean and tidy, this is a very family-friendly choice.

PARC NATURAL MONDRAGÓ ★
(159 D4–5) (ⓜ N11)

The Cala Mondragó with fine sand and turquoise water owes its protected status to a GOB initiative. There is only sparse housing around the bay. At the height of summer it can get very busy here indeed! The neighbouring Cala S'Amarador is accessed from Santanyí. An information centre (tel. 9 71 18 10 22 | daily 9am–4pm) provides information about the natural park which is home to rare and endangered species. You can explore the park on foot or by bike. 5 km (3.1 miles) east of Santanyí

LOW BUDGET

The town hall of the Llucmajor community has provided free walking tours, cycling and hiking routes in four languages to download from visitllucmajor.com/en

You normally would have to pay admission to listen to an organ concert at ● Sant Andreu (see p. 90), the village church of Santanyí. You can listen for free on Wednesdays and Saturdays at 12:30 pm.

S'ALQUERÍA BLANCA
(159 D4) (*山 N10*)

Do take a rest in this sleepy village, sit down in the tiny vilage square in the *Bar Nou* or the r estaurant *Sa Plaça* and while away the hours. Next door: *Tante Emma*, village shop and bakery – so called because the three owners are German. *5 km/3.1 miles northeast*

SES SALINES

(158 B5) (*山 L11*) **Once a sleepy village, Ses Salines (pop. 5100 including all the surrounding farms) at the very bottom of the hot south has awakened from its Sleeping Beauty slumber.**

The town benefits from its golden sandy beaches – some of which are protected – and the hotel resort of Colònia de Sant Jordi, as well as from the salt lakes. The huge *S'Avall* estate belonging to the March banking family also forms part of the municipality. Today, some good restaurants and shops have opened up along the thoroughfare.

SIGHTSEEING

BOTANICACTUS
With over 10,000 types of cacti from all over the world, and an extensive Mediterranean habitat, the complex, covering 5000 m^2, claims to be Europe's largest botanical gardens. What is certainly true is that since its opening in 1989, the garden with its artificial lake and restaurant has become a refreshing oasis in the hot south. *At the exit of the village going in the direction of Santanyí (Ma6100) | www.botanicactus.com | daily Nov–Feb 10:30am–4:30pm, March 9am–6pm, April–Aug 9am–7:30pm, Sept–Oct 9am–7pm | admission 10.50 euros*

FOOD & DRINK

ES PINARET
Sit in this cosy terrace restaurant in a pine cove while being served mediterranean or Asian cuisine. Barbecues in the summer. *Ctra. Ses Salines–Colònia Sant Jordi, km 10 | tel. 9 71 64 92 30 | www.es-pinaret.de | April–Oct Wed–Mon, Nov–March Fri/Sat 7pm–11pm, Sun 1pm–10pm | Budget–Moderate*

WHERE TO STAY

CA'N BONICO
2009 saw the opening of this fancy new hotel, converted from a 13th-century manor house right in the heart of the village. The 28 classy rooms and suites are resplendently white on white with just a few dots of colour. There's also a swimming pool and a good restaurant with terrace. *Placa Sant Bartomeu 8 | tel. 9 71 64 90 22 | www.hotelcanbonico.com | Moderate–Expensive*

WHERE TO GO

COLÒNIA DE SANT JORDI
(158 A5) (*山 K11*)

Particularly pretty it ain't, this hub of tourist accommodation and second homes 5.5 km (3.4 miles) south of Ses Salines. But the colourful little harbour provides a romantic touch; this is the starting point for walks to the unspoilt beaches of *Es Dolç* and the dream beaches of *Es Carbó* and *ses Roquetes* further to the southeast.

A young Mallorcan woman prepares excellent food with a lot of passion at the restaurant *Sal de Cocó (Moll de Pescadors | tel. 9 71 65 52 25 | www.restaurant saldecoco.com | closed Tue | Moderate)* on the harbour. The dishes with freshly caught fish are expecially tasty. But af-

The Cabrera islands belong to nature. But visitors are always welcome

ter the main course you should still leave some room for the dessert.

The port is the starting point for charming day trips by boat to ★ 🌐 *Cabrera,* the protected archipelago which can be glimpsed from the shore, boasting a castle and interesting endemic flora and fauna. An excursion with *Excursions a Cabrera (tel. 9 71 64 90 34 | www.excursionsacabrera.es)* costs from 40 euros (add 9 euros to include lunch) and includes a swim in the Blue Grotto – memories for some maybe of Capri? – and a guided tour of the castle. No time for that? How about looking through a window into Cabrera's underwater world instead? At the *national park's visitor centre (C/ Gabriel Roca | cvcabrera.es | daily 10am–2pm, 3pm–6pm| admission 8 euros)* at the town's exit you can dive down into the seawater aquarium in a INSIDER TIP **panorama lift** to look barracudas in the eye. After that, you can head up to the ☆ lookout tower. But don't run upstairs too quickly: take a break and have a look at the maritime wall mosaic first.

SALINES D'ES TRENC
(158 A–B 4–5) (*ⓜ K11*)

Dazzling white mountains in the middle of the open plains of the island's south? That is not a Fata Morgana, but a centuries-old saltworks whose high salt hills can already be spotted from afar. In the area along the road to Es Trenc, you can enjoy a play of colours in the summer: pink water, white salt mountains and blue sky. In the cold season, many migratory birds come here; from August to April, flamingos stalk through the water. In the summer you can watch the salt harvest. But don't forget a hat and sunglasses! You can get a coffee at the hippie bar and salty souvenirs at the checkout after the guided tour. *Guided tours 8 euros, English-language tours only after registration by phone. | Ctra. Campos–Colònia de Sant Jordi km 8.7 | tel. 9 71 65 53 06 | www.salinasdestrenc.com*

THE CENTRE

Es Pla, "the plain", is what they call the centre of the island. At the beginning of the 1970s, Mallorca's former cereal basket entered a crisis, but by now the island's centre has found a new identity in organic farming, crafts and viniculture. Today, excellent wines are made in bodegas in Petra *(Miquel Oliver, Can Coleto)*, Algaida *(Can Majoral)*, Porreres *(Mesquida Mora)* or Felanitx *(4 Kilos)*. For some resident farmers, the late 1980s saw the appearance of the magic words *agroturisme* and *turismo rural*, turning many a local farmer into a part-time hotelier. The softly undulating landscape is crisscrossed by narrow tarmac roads connecting all villages. This is an area for discovering disused wells, pretty wayside crosses and vicarages, as well as chapels,

hermitages and monasteries. Whilst the now widened Ma15 from Palma to Manacor has to contend with a lot of traffic, it still qualifies as a picturesque holiday road, serving rewarding destinations such as Algaida, Montuïri and Vilafranca along the way.

ALGAIDA

(157 E2) *(🗺 J7)* The first thing both locals and tourists notice in the Pla's largest municipality (pop. 4500) is the number of restaurants along the Ma15: it is not for nothing that Algaida is known as "foodie town".

The restaurants serve good Mallorcan cuisine in an old tradition: stagecoach-

A fertile plain and gentle hills: a chance to experience Mallorcan day-to-day life off the beaten tourist track

es once stopped here. The town itself is rather unspectacular.

SIGHTSEEING

VIDRIOS DE ARTE GORDIOLA ●
The island's oldest glass-blowing establishment has been going since 1719; it can be found at the westerly exit of town, on the Ma15 at kilometre 19. You can watch the glass blowers at work and visit the attached glass museum. *www.gordiola.com* | *shop: Mon–Sat 9am–7pm, Sun 9:30am–1:30pm, museum: Mon–Fri 9am–1pm, 3pm–6pm, Sat 9am–noon*

FOOD & DRINK

CAL DIMONI
Huge, rustic and very Mallorcan: this is a veteran amongst Algaida's eateries. On a Sunday though it often gets horrendously busy! | *On the Ma15 at km 21* | *tel. 9 71 66 50 35* | *www.restaurantecaldimoni.com* | *closed Wed* | *Moderate*

A fantastic view at the Santuari de Nostra Senyora de Cura

HOSTAL D'ALGAIDA ●

Cosy restaurant-cum-shop selling its own products, regional cuisine, good ambiance, regional cuisine. A place to try *pa amb oli* – with ham, cheese, pickled samphire, capers and olives. *Ma15 at km 21 | tel. 971665109 | daily | Budget–Moderate*

WHERE TO STAY

APARTAMENTS RURALS RAIMS

Manor house with picturesque patio and pool, offering one suite and four apartments on the edge of town; dinner for residents. *C/ Ribera 24 | tel. 971665157 | www.finca-raims.com | Moderate–Expensive*

WHERE TO GO

PUIG DE RANDA ★ (157 E3) (𝄡 J8)

At 542 m/1778 ft, Mallorca's only table mountain is the highest elevation on the Pla. It is worth strolling through the cobbled alleyways in the village of *Randa* (pop. 110), which sits at the foot of the

mountain. Above Randa, the mountain road leads first of all to the ✿ *Santuari de Nostra Senyora de Gràcia,* the lowest of three monasteries. The abandoned 15th-century hermitage with sweeping views across the plain from Llucmajor to the archipelago of Cabrera has been restored, the sandstone rock stabilised, and parking spaces made available. About 1 km (0.6 mile) uphill, the *Santuari de Sant Honorat* was founded at the end of the 14th century and is inhabited by monks to this day. The only part that is accessible is the 17th-century chapel. At first glimpse, the anticipated "wow" factor of the ascent is lessened somewhat by radar masts on the hilltop, but the sweeping views from the ✿ terrace of the *Santuari de Nostra Senyora de Cura* at the summit more than make up for it. In terms of cultural history, the last-named is the most important of the three monasteries. In 1263, the Santuari was the chosen retreat of Ramón Llull after he gave up his hedonistic life at the Mallorcan court. In all, Llull wrote 265 works, most of them in Catalan, elevating it to a language of literature. He researched, taught and proselytised all over the world. "Love makes the independent its servant and gives slaves freedom": This Llull quote – immortalised on his monument in Palma – speaks for the open-minded spirit of this great thinker and missionary.

Today, the classroom where grammar was taught in the old school of Cura on the mountain houses a *Ramón Llull Museum (daily 10am–6pm)*. Make sure you try the INSIDER TIP Licor Randa, a herbal liqueur which you can only get up here! The simple option for staying overnight and getting something to eat is one of the 33 former monastery cells *(tel. 9 71 12 02 60 | Budget)*. For more creature comforts, choose the *Es Recó de Randa* hotel *(25 rooms and suites | tel. 9 71 66 09 97 | www.esrecoderanda.com | Expensive)* at the foot of the mountain, with spectacular views from the ☀ terrace. A swimming pool and a fine Mallorcan restaurant are all part of the package. *4 km (2.5 miles) south of Algaida*

INCA

(148 A5) (⊍ J5) **Inca, Mallorca's fourth-largest municipality (pop. 30,600) is much more interesting than its reputation would have it.**

Although the town suffers from urban spread at the edges, it is all the prettier in the centre, with a pedestrianised zone, leafy squares and several good bars, in particular between the Plaça Santa Major, which is fringed by cafés, and the town hall square. The town, since the Catalan conquest a centre of the shoemaking profession, is today still well known for its leather goods factories; their shops however are all located outside the town centre. Excellent bakeries beckon in the extensive pedestrian zone; another good choice are

the *cellers*, cellar pubs serving down-to-earth local cuisine. The weekly market on a Thursday might be the island's largest, but it is also very touristy; in terms of charm, the annual *dijous bou*, the island's largest agricultural fair on the second Thursday in November, has more to offer.

FOOD & DRINK/ WHERE TO STAY

ES CASTELL

Small fine finca hotel with remote location around Inca. ☀ INSIDER TIP Spectacular far-reaching views from the Migdia junior suite for 210 euros! *11 rooms | at Binibona | tel. 9 71 87 51 54 | www.fincaescastell.com | Expensive*

CELLERS

The most famous and most expensive one is the pretty *Can Amer (C/ Pau 39 | www.celler-canamer.es)*. The offerings of *Sa Travessa* in the same street and boasting a patio are fairly original, while the

MARCO POLO HIGHLIGHTS

⭐ **Puig de Randa**
Dream views from Mallorca's only table mountain → p. 98

⭐ **Els Calderers**
Deep insights into the feudal way of life in the olden days, for young and old → p. 102

⭐ **Ermita de Bonany**
Meet a peasant Madonna and enjoy sweeping views across the heart of the island → p. 103

⭐ **Sineu market**
Every Wednesday: shop at Mallorca's largest market → p. 105

mid-range *Can Ripoll (C/ Armengol 4)* offers authentic fare. *Can Marrón (C/ Rector Rayo 7)* offers genuinely traditional cuisine among old wine barrels.

ELS TRES CARAGOLS ⚫

Local organic cuisine in the restaurant of the *Fábrica Ramis,* a former leather factory and today a cultural centre. *Gran Vía de Colón 28 | tel. 9 71 50 19 00 | www.fab bricaramis.com | daily | Budget–Moderate*

SHOPPING

Asinca, Camper, Farrutx, Lotusse and *Munper* are the leather goods factories that sell their wares along the Carretera Palma–Inca. For an extensive shopping

LOW BUDGET

A good-value means of transport is the train. The route Palma – Inca – Manacor starts in Palma at the *Estació Intermodal (underneath Plaça Espanya)* with stops of interest to tourists such as Sineu or Petra. A Palma–Manacor trip for instance costs 3.55 euros.

The *birthplace of Juníper Serra* (see p. 103) in Petra is only one of six religious hotspots which you can visit with the combined ticket of ⚫ *Spiritual Mallorca (www.spiritua lmallorca.com)*. For 15 euros, you have access to La Seu Cathedral (see p. 35), *La Porciúncula* church and *La Real* monastery in Palma, *Lluc* monastery (see p. 75) and *Cura* monastery (see p. 98) on the Puig de Randa.

tour head for the traffic-calmed centre around the market square at Carrer Pau where there are more than 200 shops.

WHERE TO GO

ALARÓ (152 B2) *(𝄢 G–H5)*
11 km (6.8 miles) west of Inca, Alaró (pop. 5200) is a welcoming village of Arabic origins surrounded by gardens and almond tree groves. At the centre, the market square with church, town hall and bars also boasts the ⚫ *Ca na Juanita* bakery founded in 1910 and famous for its *ensaïmadas.* Centrally on the market square, the comfortable hotel *Can Xim (8 rooms | tel. 9 71 87 91 17 | www.canx im.com | Moderate)* offers a pool, a garden and its own terrace restaurant *Traffic.* The mountain restaurant *Es Verger (tel. 9 71 18 21 26 | daily | Budget)* above Alaró is famous for its lamb shoulder and snails by a cosy fireplace. From here you can hike to the ⚅ *Castell d'Alaró* in about an hour where there is a simple *restaurant (tel. 9 71 94 05 03 | daily | Budget)*.

BINISSALEM (152 C3) *(𝄢 H5)*
The prettily restored small town (pop. 7600) 6 km (3.7 miles) southwest of Inca was the first region on Mallorca whose wines were entitled to call themselves "Denominació de origen" for their certified origin. The largest local bodega is the *Bodega José L. Ferrer (tel. 9 71 51 10 50 | www.vinosferrer.com)* on the road to Palma. By phone, you can book guided tours *(Mon–Fri 11am–4:30pm | 14 euros per person)* through the cellar and the vineyards, including a tasting.

S'OLIERA DE SON CATIU (153 E3) *(𝄢 K6)*
The new, very modern *tafona* (oil mill) 12 km (7.5 miles) northwest of Sineu with a large restaurant with INSIDER TIP ▶ excel-

Windmills and wheat fields: the village of Montuïri is a rural idyll

lent *pa amb olis* (8–14 euros) and sale of Mallorcan products is well worth visiting. In early October, farmers and finca owners bring in olives by the sackful. Ask staff to show you how the olives are processed, and the machines. *Ctra. Llubí–Inca at the roundabout (Ctra. Muro) | tel. 9 71 50 00 01 | www.soncatiu.com*

MONTUÏRI

(157 F2) (*M K7*) **With its sturdy parish church and 19 mill towers, testimonies to a long agricultural tradition, this stretched-out hilltop village (pop. 2600) of Arabic origin is pretty as a picture.**

Today, the small town owes its fame to breeding partridges and to the fact that in 1995 the famous *Perlas Orquídeas* pearl company transferred one of its factories here. A stroll around the *plaça* (with the weekly market on a Monday) leads past well-preserved houses, wells, wayside crosses and mills, as well as past the broad flight of steps in front of the parish church of *Sant Bartomeu*, dating back to the 16th to 18th centuries. In the town hall awaits a ready-made alternative to beach tourism: a one-hour stroll to the town's most beautiful windmills, with an introduction to the history of grain milling from the second century BC onwards.

HORTELLA D'EN COTANET 〰️

Spacious, family-run country inn located between Montuïri, Sant Joan and Vilafranca and serving local dishes. While you wait for your dinner on the terrace, your gaze can travel over fields and forests. In the summer, jazz concerts are performed on the meadow. *Ctra. Palma–Manacor, exit 34 | tel. 9 71 83 21 43 | www.hortelladencotanet.com | closed Mon; Nov–May Tue–Thu and Sun evenings by appointment only | Budget*

These grapes have never encountered any chemicals: Bodega Jaume Mesquida

WHERE TO STAY

ES PUIG MOLTÓ ☼

18 picture-perfect rooms, suites and apartments in a restored estate with pool and a magnificent view across the surrounding farmland. *Ctra. Pina–Montuiri at km 3 | tel. 9 71 18 17 58 | www.es puigmolto.com | Expensive*

WHERE TO GO

ELS CALDERERS ★ (153 F5) (*Ⓜ L7*)

The fortification-like manor house, with its own chapel, wine cellar, stables, servants' quarters and aristocratic salons, conveys an idea of former feudal life. Stroll around the more than 300 years old walls or participate yourself, e.g. by feeding the animals. *7 km (4.4 miles) east at Sant Joan on the Ma15, km 37 (signposted) | www.elscalderes.com | April–Oct 10am–6pm, Nov–March 10am–5pm | admission 9 euros*

PORRERES (153 E6) (*Ⓜ L8*)

A widening of the approach roads has made this small town 7 km (4.4 miles) south of Montuï (pop. 5300) more accessible. The weekly market on a Tuesday is ideal for a visit. Don't miss the astounding exhibition of contemporary art in the old hospital building, the *Museu i Fons Artístic (C/ d'Agustí Font | Tue/Sun 11am–1pm, Fri/Sat 11am–1pm, 6pm–8pm, summer 7pm–9pm)*. Among the 300 objects are two Dalís. The rose window and bell tower of the parish church on the market square are impressive too. Right next to the church, the *Centre (tel. 9 71 16 83 72 | daily | Budget)*, a former theatre, today functions as a rustic restaurant. The rural hotel complex of *Sa Bassa Rotja (Camino Sa Pedrera | tel. 9 71 16 82 25 | www.sabas sarotja.com | Expensive)* with 25 luxury suites, two pools, beauty farm and restaurant lies outside the town. These days, Porreres has returned to making a living from its wine. Right in the heart of the town, you can visit the ◯ bodega *Jaume Mesquida (C/ Vileta 7 | tel. 9 71 64 71 06 | www.jaumemesquida.com)*. This vineyard does not use chemical pesticides or fertilisers. The bodega offers a variety of options ranging from a simple wine tasting to an extended lunch or dinner. Book your tasting or guided tour via email: *info@weimertandfriend.com*.

PETRA

(154 A4) (*Ⓜ M6–7*) **The alleyways of this sleepy village (pop. 2700) were laid out in their chequer-board pattern under Jaume I.**

Petra was called "The Luminous One" by its Arabic founders in an allusion to its Jordanian sister. Petra's second great claim to fame is its most famous son, Fra Juníper Serra, Franciscan monk and missionary, who was canonised in 2015 by Pope Francis. From 1769 onwards Serra founded 21 mission stations in California, which were to develop into cities with millions of inhabitants, such as San Francisco and Los Angeles.

SIGHTSEEING

CASA NATAL I MUSEU JUNÍPER SERRA

Find out the story of the life of the missionary and saint (1713–84) in the house of his birth and the museum. *C/ Barracar/C/ Fra Juníper Serra | www.fundacioncasaserra.org | Tue/Thu 10am–2pm or pre-book via mobile tel. 6 64 36 67 22 | admission free, donations customary*

BODEGA MIQUEL OLIVER

With this bodega Petra can boast one of the most famous on the island. Today, daughter Pilar Oliver rules the roost as enologist and cellar mistress. Her dry Muscat has been crowned the best white wine in Spain. Signposted. *Ctra. Petra–Santa Margalida, km 1.8 | www.miqueloliver.com*

FOOD & DRINK/ WHERE TO STAY

ES CELLER

There's no place quite as cosily old-fashioned and with such unique ambiance as this cellar tavern in the heart of the town. The quality of the dishes unfortunately oscillates between excellent and mediocre. *C/ de l'Hospital 46 | signposted | tel. 9 71 56 10 56 | closed Mon | Budget*

SA PLAÇA PETRA

Tiny village hotel with lovingly decorated restaurant and inviting patio. The menu is a little disappointing, not so the three pretty rooms at a fair price. *Plaça Ramón Llull 4 | tel. 9 71 56 16 46 | www.petithotel petra.com | Moderate*

WHERE TO GO

ARIANY (154 A3) (*M6*)

This small village (pop. 900) 2.5 km (1.5 mile) north of Petra only achieved independence from its neighbour in 1982. The village's heart is its church, whose dreamy front garden, full of blooms and boasting sweeping views, is well worth a stop. The restaurant *Ses Torres (daily | Budget)* at the big roundabout of Ariany is a huge pit stop for truck drivers and day trippers where you can get good tapas and a good-value set meal.

ERMITA DE BONANY ★ (154 A5) (*L7*)

A detour to the monastery is worth doing for the chubby-faced Madonna figure dating back to the 8th century and the panoramic view alone. The monastery owes its name (Good Year) to the end of a period of

FOR BOOKWORMS

A Winter in Mallorca – describes the love-hate relationship that George Sand had with the island and its inhabitants in the winter of 1838–39, which she experienced – and suffered – with her lover Frédéric Chopin in Palma and Valldemossa: a must-read

The Vacationers – Emma Straub's novel (2014) is set in a hot summer in a remote holiday home at the foot of the Tramuntana mountains where a rather dysfunctional extended family spends their holidays and all family members face problems of their own

The market has been a Sineu institution for 700 years

severe drought. At the entrance, tiled images are a reminder of the long-awaited rain and the rich harvest that followed. There is also a fantastic picnic area under shade-giving trees. *4 km (2.5 miles) south of Petra*

SENCELLES

(152–153 C–D4) (*⋔ J6*) The charm of this region to the west of the Pla lies in the many hamlets surrounding Sencelles, all well restored.

In Sencelles itself (pop. 2900), the village at the heart of all the others, the traditions of making bagpipes and of cultivating figs have been preserved to this day. However, the village has now become first and foremost a choice spot for foreigners' second homes.

FOOD & DRINK

SA CUINA DE N'AINA

A Mallorcan family business in which mother Aina cooks alongside her daughter Virginia and her daughter-in-law Laura whilst father José takes care of business and son David heads up the waitstaff. Good suckling pig. *C/ Rafal 31 | tel. 9 71 87 29 92 | www.sacuinadenaina. com | closed Tue | Moderate*

WHERE TO STAY

SA TORRE

The friendly owners of this 300-year-old rural estate offer six units, with two pools, in the hamlet *Ses Alqueríes*, 2 km (1.2 mile) away. The four-course tasting menu for 39 euros is served in the property's prettiest room: its INSIDER TIP wine cellar, with walls 10 m/33 ft high; it feels like eating on a film set. *Tel. 9 71 14 40 11 | www.sa-torre.com | closed Mon | Expensive*

WHERE TO GO

COSTITX (153 D3) (*⋔ K6*)

Situated 4.5 km (2.8 miles) further east in a pretty position on a hill, the village (pop. 1000) was made famous by the find, in 1894, of three bronze bull heads dating back to Talaiotic times. The pieces are exhibited in the *Museu de Ciències (www.museuciencies.com | Sept–July Tue–Fri 9am–1pm; 2nd and 3rd weekend of the month 9:30am–1pm | admission 3 euros)* in the *Casal de Cultura (at the village entrance coming from Sencelles)*. Near Costitx you can also find the Balearics' only observatory *(www.oam. es)*, in existence since 1991. In the *Mallorca Planetarium* next door *(www.mallorcaplanetarium.com | Fri/Sat 8pm | admission 10 euros)* visitors can experience over 6000 virtual stars and may view the real thing through telescopes. A replica of the Apollo 11 spacecraft is also on view.

SINEU

(153 E3–4) (_ɰ_ K–L6) **Of all the villages in the centre, Sineu (pop. 3300) is the most famous. This is mainly due to the ⭐ market every Wednesday, which has been held since 1306 and is the largest of its kind on Mallorca.**
The best time to visit the market is very early in the morning, before the tourist buses arrive. But there is much more to Sineu: of Talaiotic-Roman origin and later one of the island's six main Arabic settlements, in medieval times Sineu was chosen by King Jaume II as his residence.

SIGHTSEEING

MARE DE DEU DELS ANGELS
A broad flight of steps leads up to the massive church, which reveals a surprisingly delicate-looking interior. A winged bronze lion guards the church with its 16th-century statue of the Virgin. The *Casa Rectoral* (rectory) *(Wed at market times)* exhibits nearly 800 ceramics dating back to the 12th and 13th centuries.

INSIDER TIP ▸ VI–ÉS
Young Mallorcan gallerists have turned the old railway station in Sineu into a sight worth seeing that features art, fine dining and lively cultural offerings in a pleasant atmosphere. Cooking and dance courses (swing and salsa), wine tastings and live concerts are offered regularly. *C/ Estació 2 | tel. 9 71 52 10 34 | www.viesgastroart.com | Mon/Tue, Thu–Sat 7pm–11pm, Wed all day*

FOOD & DRINK

CELLER ES GROP
Small and cosy, friendly service. *C/ Major 18 | pedestrian area | tel. 9 71 52 01 87 | closed Sun evening and Mon | Budget*

CELLER SON TOREO
Less romantic, but very authentic, and popular with the locals. *C/ Son Torelló 1 | tel. 9 71 52 01 38 | closed Mon | Budget*

WHERE TO STAY

INSIDER TIP ▸ SA CASA ROTJA
Beautifully restored farmhouse 4 km/2.5 miles north of Sineu, offering seven simple holiday flats, a salon as well as a garden, a pool and a barbecue area. An ideal place to spend your holiday in a natural environment with your family. *Ctra. Sineu–Muro | tel. 9 71 18 52 90 | www.sacasarotja.com | Budget*

DAICA
Small hotel by the chuch in the neighbouring village of Llubí. With only three rooms, a calm restaurant with freshly prepared Mallorcan dishes and a pretty courtyard, this hotel is for guests wanting to get to know the quiet Mallorca. *Tel. 9 971 52 25 67 | www.daica.es | Moderate*

DISCOVERY TOURS

1

MALLORCA AT A GLANCE

START: **1** Palma END: **1** Palma	**6 days** Driving time (without stops) 7½ hours
Distance: 🚗 400 km/249 miles	

COSTS: accommodation for 5 nights (double room with breakfast) 600 euros; boat ride to **4** Sa Dragonera 12 euros; admission to the **6** Valldemossa Charterhouse 8.50 euros, bike rental 10 euros per day

WHAT TO PACK: swim gear, diving mask, water shoes, hiking boots, sun protection, trail maps

IMPORTANT TIPS: You can only visit the island of **4** Sa Dragonera from April to October.

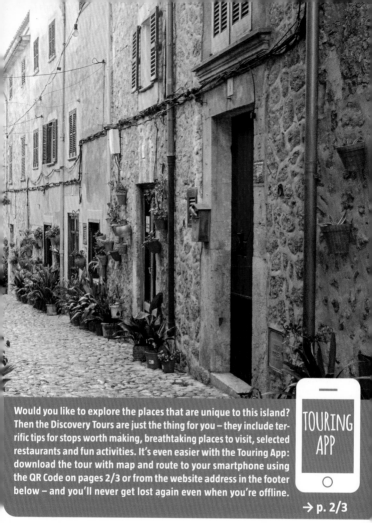

Would you like to explore the places that are unique to this island? Then the Discovery Tours are just the thing for you – they include terrific tips for stops worth making, breathtaking places to visit, selected restaurants and fun activities. It's even easier with the Touring App: download the tour with map and route to your smartphone using the QR Code on pages 2/3 or from the website address in the footer below – and you'll never get lost again even when you're offline.

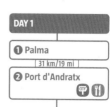

TOURING APP

→ p. 2/3

From protected nature reserves with hardly any people to the party crowds, the rocky coast and the interior plateaus, this round-trip tour will introduce you to all the different faces of the island.

Regardless of whether arriving by ship or aeroplane, almost everyone's first stop is the lively capital city of ❶ Palma → p. 32. But, this time around, save the capital itself for later and just pick up a rental car so that you can get to know the island as a whole first. **Take the Ma1** to ❷ Port d'Andratx → p. 46. Stroll for a bit

DAY 1

❶ Palma
  31 km/19 mi
❷ Port d'Andratx

Photo: A street in the mountain village of Valdemossa

along the harbour and have a look at the yachts and fishing boats before stopping for a bite to eat at one of the many restaurants. Then drive on to the peaceful seaside resort of **3 Sant Elm → p. 49**. Boats depart from here that will ferry you across to the unspoilt island of **4 Sa Dragonera** with its many birds and lizards. The crossing only takes about 20 minutes, but plan at least three hours for this little excursion. Once you are back on the mainland, follow the **curvy Ma10** to the sleepy hillside village of **5 Estellencs → p. 49**. The village clings to the steep coastal cliffs, offering a view of the sea from almost everywhere. You can spend the night at **Petit Hotel Sa Plana** *(6 rooms | C/*

d'Eusebi Pascual 3 | tel. 9 71 61 86 66 | www.saplana. com | *Moderate*).

On the next day, head off to **⑥ Valldemossa → p. 58.** A visit to the **charterhouse** is a must. Afterwards, treat yourself to a sweet and delicious INSIDER TIP *coca de patata*, which you can buy at just about every bakery, and meander through the lower village. The next part of the drive is quite spectacular with the sea to the left and olive groves and rock walls to the right. Stop at the **⑦ Son Marroig estate → p. 51** and tour the idyllic gardens before driving past the picture-perfect houses nestled into the hills in **⑧ Deià → p. 50.** Continue on to **⑨ Sóller → p. 54** where you can relax and enjoy an ice cream on the patio of the **Fàbrica de Gelats.** Book a nice room for the night in the part of town on the sea called Port de Sóller at the very fine **Hotel Espléndido.**

After breakfast, follow the **Ma10** up to the highest mountains on the island. As you curve up the road, the views are amazing. You will pass two reservoir lakes before you come to the **⑩ Lluc Monastery → p. 75,** which is home to the famous "Black Madonna". Drive down through the forests of holm oaks to the country town of Pollença. Your next destination is the **⑪ Formentor Peninsula → p. 74.** Stop at the **Mirador** and enjoy the fantastic view before taking a break for a coffee in the garden of the hotel **Barceló Formentor.** When your cup is empty, it's time to drive on to the medieval walls of **⑫ Alcúdia → p. 60.** Check into your room at **Ca'n Pere Hotel** (8 rooms | C/ den Serra 12 | tel. 9 71 54 52 43 | www.hotelcanpere.com | *Moderate*) and then stroll through the beautifully restored houses in the centre of town.

On the next day, embark on a worthwhile excursion up the cliffs to the **⑬ Ermita de la Victoria → p. 64.** You can go for a swim right below the hermitage on the narrow pebble beach of **S'Illot.** Get on the **Ma12** to drive on to **⑭ Can Picafort → p. 69.** Check into your hotel of choice and then treat yourself to a nice lunch. In the afternoon, rent a bike at **Mallorca on Bike** (Ctra. Artá–Port d'Alcùdia 65 B | mobile tel. 6 96 38 73 44 | www.mallor caonbike.com | daily 9am–noon, 5pm–7pm and by arrangement). Hop on and **cycle along the Ma12** until you come to a former country estate that now houses a **⑮ museum of island history.** Walk **along the trail to**

DAY 2
24 km/15 mi
⑥ Valldemossa
8 km/5 mi
⑦ Son Marroig
4 km/2.5 mi
⑧ Deià
11 km/6.8 mi
⑨ Sóller

DAY 3
40 km/25 mi
⑩ Lluc Monastery
30 km/19 mi
⑪ Formentor Peninsula
24 km/15 mi
⑫ Alcúdia

DAY 4
7 km/4.4 mi
⑬ Ermita de la Victoria
17 km/10.5 mi
⑭ Can Picafort
5 km/3.2 mi
⑮ museum of island history

(2.4 km / 1.5 mi)

⑯ Son Real 🏛️ 🏖️

(9.5 km / 6 mi)

⑰ Es Casal 🍴

DAY 5

(26 km / 16 mi)

⑱ Ses Països 🏛️

(2 km / 1.2 mi)

⑲ Artà 🏛️ ☕ 🍴

(33 km / 20.5 mi)

⑳ Petra 🏪 🏛️

(25 km / 15.5 mi)

㉑ Sant Salvador 🍃 ☕ 🛏️

DAY 6

(21 km / 13 mi)

㉒ Campos 🏠 ☕ 🏛️

(14 km / 8.7 mi)

㉓ Llucmajor 🏪 🍴 🛍️

⑯ **Son Real → p. 69**, the largest Talaiotic city of the dead. This necropolis sits directly by the sea, so take the time for a quick swim. Return to Can Picafort and turn in your bike. In the evening, a drive to the gourmet restaurant ⑰ **Es Casal** *(Ctra. Santa Margalida–Alcúdia km 1.8 | tel. 9 71 85 27 32 | www.casal-santaeulalia.com | Expensive)* is definitely worthwhile.

Continue exploring Talaiotic culture on the following day with a visit to ⑱ **Ses Països**, an impressive settlement dating back to this period. In the lovely country town of ⑲ **Artà → p. 64**, **start at the parish church and follow the Way of the Cross lined by cypresses up to the** fortress to enjoy the amazing panoramic view. After a break for lunch, **drive along the Ma15 into the interior of the island. Pass through Manacor and then turn onto the Ma3320**, which will bring you to the Es Pla plateau and the little town of ⑳ **Petra → p. 102**. Explore its decoratively tiled lanes and museum dedicated to Friar Juníper Serra, the founder of many Californian cities. Take the **Ma3310, the Ma5110 and the Ma5111** through fields of wheat and vineyards to Felanitx and then continue on the **Ma4010**. Turn onto the narrow **serpentine road** that leads up to the holy mountain of ㉑ **Sant Salvador → p. 81** and spend a wonderful night at the **Petit Hotel**.

Depart Sant Salvador the next morning and drive back to **Felanitx to access the PM512**, which will take you to the farming village of ㉒ **Campos → p. 86**. If you want to interact with the locals, pop into the bakery **Forn Ca'n Nadal** *(C/ Estrelles 22)* for some crunchy bread fresh from the wood-fired oven and tasty *ensaimadas* (a kind of lardy cake). Or stop and visit the friendly artist **Miquela Vidal** *(C/ Pare Alzina 7 | tel. 9 71 65 20 10 | www.miquelavidal.com)*. She opens her home/atelier on market Saturdays and at other times if you ask in advance. Not only can you buy art and antiques, but also you can see her wonderfully renovated house in the village. Afterwards, walk past the stalls of the weekly market in Campos. The village has carved a name for itself as a little rummage haven with plenty of bric-a-brac, bits and bobs, and unique souvenirs.

Drive on to ㉓ **Llucmajor → p. 89**. This large island municipality is not particularly beautiful, but it still has lots to offer visitors. **Park your car as quickly as you can on the thoroughfare** and ask your way to the busy **village square (Plaça**

An abandoned monastery sits atop the mountain of Sant Salvador (509 m/1670 ft)

Espanya) nearby. The square is lined with outdoor cafés and small restaurants that are perfect for people-watching in a relaxed atmosphere. Some of the little shops are rather quaint, but others are quite stylish. You can download a guide for a cultural walking tour in four languages from the town hall's website *(www.visitllucmajor.com)*.

It is only a stone's throw from Llucmajor to ㉔ **Platja de Palma** → p. 44 **on the Ma19**. The beach begins in Arenal, but the bay stretches over 10 km (6 miles) to the outskirts of Palma. If you want to take just one look at the infamous **Ballermann**, the beach section 6 so popular among German tourists looking to party day and night, **park in Arenal** and walk for about a half an hour **along the beach promenade towards Palma**. On the **street named Pare Bartomeu Salvà**, you will find the German watering hole called the **Bierkönig** in the midst of the legendary party area. If you want to stop for a bite to eat on the way back to the car, be wary of the tourist traps. A recommendable restaurant is **Casa do Pulpo** *(C/ Terral 44 | tel. 9 71 44 15 77 | Budget–Moderate)*. The round-trip route has now brought you back to ❶ **Palma**. Plan on spending a few days exploring the capital – you won't be disappointed!

2 A WALK IN THE FOOTSTEPS OF SMUGGLERS

START: ❶ Banyalbufar	½ day
END: ❶ Banyalbufar	Walking time
	(without stops)
Distance: easy	3 hours
⟷ 12 km/7.5 mi .ıl Height: 150 m/492 ft	

WHAT TO PACK: swim gear (plus water shoes and a diving mask), sun protection, picnic lunch, drinking water

IMPORTANT TIPS: the rocky beach of ❸ Port des Canonge is great for snorkelling, but sometimes you have to watch out for the jellyfish. There are no toilets or places to eat/drink at the beach.

This easy hike follows an old smugglers' path from Banyalbufar to the harbour of Port des Canonge and back. The blue sea far down below sparkles between the green tree branches. Depending on the time of year, the path is lined by blooming heather, the ripe red fruit of strawberry trees or the green *ginebrós*, the juniper berries that are destilled to make fine gins.

❶ Banyalbufar

4.5 km/2.8mi

eave the mountain village of ❶ **Banyalbufar → p. 49 and drive eastwards. On the Ma10, in an S-curve between kilometre 85 and 86**, you will find a **car park**. It is the starting point for the day's hike. The trail is marked the entire way with arrows on wooden stakes. Thanks to the shady forest of Aleppo pines, the hike is not too strenuous on hot summer days. This path was used by smugglers during the Franco era who transported sacks of cigarettes, alcohol and coffee from the sea to their hideaways. Let your imagination run wild as you walk in their footsteps.

After just a few strides, Banyalbufar with its terraced fields of vegetables and malvasia grapes dating back to Moorish times will rise up before you. The t**rail leads through a forest of holm oaks** in which virtually extinct wood trades have been kept alive in the form of a *sitga,* a circular charcoal pile with a reed-covered hut for the charcoal burners who had to be on site day and night. Also keep a lookout for the ruins of a *forn de calç,* a lime kiln, in which limestone was fired to produce lime for whitewashing houses. Almost unnoticeably, the path **slopes down gently. Continue walking for about a half an hour** until you come to a **huge crag.** Admire the stalactites and stalagmites in the limestone and listen to rumbling sea. On days when the sea is restless, the wall amplifies the thunderous sound of the waves.

As you walk further along, you will eventually come to a point where bizarre, wildly romantic rock crags jut out over the sea far below with wind-bent pines clinging to them. White sea spray crashes onto the rocky beach as every now and then a boat crosses the broad blue horizon of the sea. Far off into the distance, try to make out the shape of the small Sa Foradada peninsula. It was here that Archduke Ludwig Salvator hit land and "discovered" Mallorca. The trail continues **downhill**, past the large, 400-year old estate of ➋ **Son Bunyola**. A British billionaire purchased the property in order to build a luxurious finca hotel on the site, but he is still waiting for a building permit to this day... Finally, the sea with its crystal clear water lies at your feet. The pebble beach is a paradise for snorkelling. Don't hesitate, just jump right in – with or without a swimsuit.

You still have a bit to go – **past myrtle bushes** – until you come to the tiny harbour town of ➌ **Port des Canonge**. At the height of summer, it is a lively place, especially at the weekend when Mallorcan daytrippers arrive. At other times of the year, it is virtually abandoned – which makes

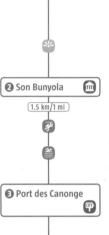

➋ Son Bunyola

1.5 km/1 mi

➌ Port des Canonge

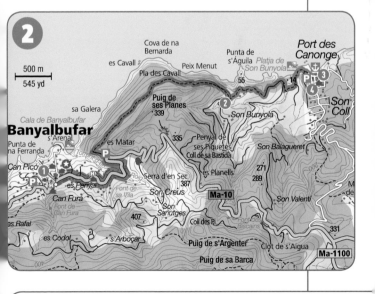

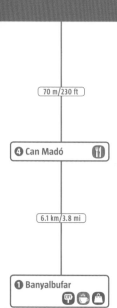

70 m / 230 ft

❹ Can Madó 🍴

6.1 km / 3.8 mi

❶ Banyalbufar
🏧 ☕ 🛍️

it all the more charming. Red rocks tower over the harbour ringed by softly rounded red stones and algae. The scent of fish and salt fill the air. Sometimes the fishermen nap in the shade of their tarpaulins. All in all, it is a peaceful place seemingly at the end of the world. If you have brought along a picnic lunch, then this is a great place to take a break and enjoy your sandwiches. If you haven't packed a lunch, walk **up the main street,** past the restaurant Toni, and grab a table at ❹ **Can Madó** *(C/ Port des Canonge | tel. 9 71 61 05 52 | Wed–Mon 10am–6pm | Moderate)*. The place is not particularly pretty, but quite down-to-earth. Order a few tapas and a glass of the excellent white house wine, watch the cats who mill about and forget for a moment that you have to **hike uphill all the way back to the car**. Nonetheless, you can rest assured knowing that you will discover entirely new vistas and lots of other things along the trail that you missed on the way down.

Don't forget to visit ❶ **Banyalbufar** → p. 49 on your return. This town nestled on the hillside is busy in summer, especially because many Mallorcans own holiday flats here. They treasure the natural beauty of the west coast with its spectacular sunsets. Good coffee and cake can be had on the main road at **Café Bellavista** *(C/ del Comte de Sallent 15)*. Malvasia wine from the village is sold next door.

Hikers on the way to the Port des Canonge

3 THE COUNTRY & ITS PEOPLE: FARMERS, VINTNERS & FISHERMEN

START: ❶ Sineu	3 days
END: ❶ Sineu	Driving time
Distance:	(without stops)
🚗 170 km/106 miles	3½ hours

COSTS: two nights' accommodation (double room with breakfast) approx. 110 euros; ❷ Els Calderers admission 8 euros; ⓫ Salines d'Es Trenc guided tour 8 euros

WHAT TO PACK: swim gear, sun protection, hiking boots

IMPORTANT TIPS: If possible, start or end in Sineu on a Wednesday to see the market. ⓫ Salines d'Es Trenc guided tour times vary; enquire beforehand at *tel. 9 71 65 53 06.*

Starting from Sineu, explore the great plateau of Es Plá before heading deep into the south. Along the way, you'll meet locals who have little to do with the tourist industry *per se.* Naturally, some fantastic beaches also await along this route.

08:30am The starting point for this tour is ❶ Sineu → p. 105 at the geographical heart of the island. Farmers from far and wide flock to the island's oldest and most important **market** held here on Wednesdays. If you get there really early, you can witness the haggling over chicks and cows or sheep and pigs. Around 10am, when entire coachloads of tourists pour into the market, you should already be on your way **7 km/4.3 miles to the south** in Sant Joan. **In the centre of the village, follow the sign to Els Calderers.** It leads to the impressive estate of ❷ Els Calderers → p. 102, which has been converted into a finca museum. A huge wine cellar attests to the former glory of the wine making trade that flourished here until the phylloxera pest hit at the turn of the 20th century. Recently, efforts have been made to revive the vineyards. An enormous granary on the upper floor marks the switchover from wine to wheat that took place over the last century and displays the estate's other agricultural products. Make sure to take advantage of the wine tastings on offer.

12:00pm As you drive **further south,** you will pass through the municipality of Vilafranca. Smoke-black-

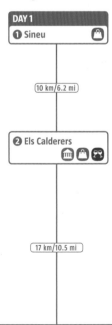

DAY 1

❶ Sineu

10 km/6.2 mi

❷ Els Calderers

17 km/10.5 mi

ened kilns and piles of *tejas* (slates) tell of the old and still practised trade of brick making. Until now, fields of wheat and plantations of trees bearing almonds, figs and carob have lined the road. But once you **cross the Ma15,** vineyards take over. The area around Petra, Porreres and Felanitx is one of the main cultivation areas white wine.

3 Felanitx 🍴 🏬 🏨

15 km/9.3 mi

01:00pm You will soon come across the country town of **3 Felanitx → p. 77** with its characteristic mill stumps. The main street, Carrer Major, is the heart of life in the town. Time for lunch? For upscale cuisine at reasonable prices, check out **Cas Solleric** *(tel. 971 58 43 80 | www. cassolleric.com | closed Mon | Moderate)* at house number 11. Afterwards, stroll down Carrer Major and explore the lovely shops such as the candle and jewellery gallery called **Candela Home** *(No. 60)* or the well-established pottery workshop **Call Vermell** at number 44.

4 Portocolom 🏬 🍸

04:00pm The next destination is **4 Portocolom → p. 80,** the harbour of Felanitx. The funnel-shaped harbour is framed by INSIDER TIP colourfully painted boat sheds belonging to the fishermen. A visit to the somewhat hidden church square in Portocolom, **Plaça Sant Jaume,** is worth the effort because it shows you the most authentic side of the town. The village bars are the place to go to have a drink alongside the locals. But, before dinner, you should walk to the **lighthouse**. It sits just about **3 km (2 miles) from the old village centre on the Punta de Sa Cresta**. It separates the narrow bay from the wide open sea and the view of the horizon is fantastic. It's an easy walk that will take less than a half an hour each way. If you've worked up an appetite, go to the harbour restaurant **Sa Sinia** *(tel. 971 82 43 23 | closed Mon | Expensive)* that serves freshly caught fish. An inexpensive hotel at the beach is the **Club Cala Marsal**.

DAY 2

30 km/19 mi

10:00am On the next morning, drive over the first foothills of the Serra de Llevant. Pass through the flower-bedecked villages of S'Horta and Calonge and, via **S'Alquería Blanca → p. 94** to the edge of Santanyí → p. 90. Follow the road sign in the direction of Cala S'Amarador/Cala Mondragó. This road, as is typical for the south of the island, is lined by dry-stone walls *(parets seques)*. It ends after 5 km (3 miles) at the gate of the

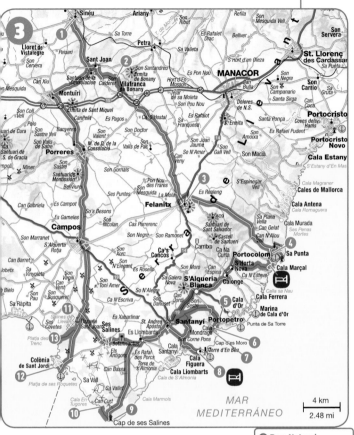

nature reserve **⑤ Parc Natural Mondragó → p. 93**. The park is home to 70 species of birds as well as rare plants and animals such as tortoises and genets. From the **Visitors' Centre** *(daily 9am–4pm)*, it is just **about 500 m (546 yds) on foot** through the fragrant pine forest to the beautiful bay of **⑥ Ses Fonts de n'Alís**, which is a popular place to swim in summer. A short **path along the rocky coast** leads to the other bay within the park, the **⑦ Cala S'Amarador**. You only have to walk about 2.5 km (1.5 miles) from here to get back to the car park. A narrow, **U-shaped trail** at the end of the Amarador beach heads through garrigue and Mediterranean forests of juniper and pines. It **starts off to the side, to the right if**

⑤ Parc Natural Mondragó

`1 km/0.6 mi`

⑥ Ses Fonts de n'Alís

`0.5 km/546 yd`

⑦ Cala S'Amarador

`14 km/8.7 mi`

Wednesday is market day in Sineu

you are looking to the sea. Hike about a half hour to the rocky coastline and through the forest **once the path curves to the right away from the sea**. The trail runs into an **asphalt road** that you should **follow to the right** to get back to Amarador beach and return to the car park.

`03:00pm` On the **way back to Santanyí, a road branches off to the left** to the resort town of ❽ **Cala Figuera → p. 92**. It is the second harbour on this route. In the afternoon, you can watch as the fishing boats return with their catches. **Stroll along the lovely Paseo Marítimo** high above the bay and stop for a bit on the way back, for example at the **Bon-Bar** with its pretty view of the harbour. A good place to spend the night is **Rocamar** *(42 rooms | tel. 9 71 64 51 25 | www.rocamarplayamar.com | Budget)*. The hotel sits openly above the sea and has its own path to the water.

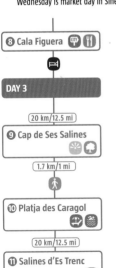

❽ Cala Figuera 🛍 🍴

🚻

DAY 3

20 km/12.5 mi

❾ Cap de Ses Salines 🏖 🌳

1.7 km/1 mi

🚶

❿ Platja des Caragol 🚻 🏊

20 km/12.5 mi

⓫ Salines d'Es Trenc 🌳

4.5 km/2.8 mi

`08:00am` On the next day, try to get an early start **from Santanyí**. Follow the **signs to Colònia de Sant Jordi and Llombards**. Shortly past Llombards, **turn left on the Ma6110** and drive for 10 km (6 miles) towards the southern tip of Mallorca. An easy hiking trail leads from the ❾ **Cap de Ses Salines** along the unspoilt coastline to the heavenly bay of ❿ INSIDER TIP **Platja des Caragol** (pack sun protection!). This beach, just like the neighbouring bay of Cala Entugores, is popular among nudist bathers. Both beaches count among the most beautiful natural beaches on the island. Enjoy an unforgettable morning swim. It takes about a half an hour on the path through the dunes, beach grass and sand to get there and back.

`11:00am` Once you're back at the car, **drive through Ses Salines** to the ⓫ **Salines d'ES Trenc → p. 95** where the island is flat and mostly treeless. Only bird calls interrupt the silence of the salt pools. On a tour you can learn interesting facts about the ecosystem of the wetlands with its many species and habitats as well as about how sea salt is harvested and produced, a process which is tightly linked to the seasons of the year.

01:30pm For a delicious lunch, head to ⑫ **Colònia de Sant Jordi** → p. 94 to the **Sal de Cocó** (*C/ Es Carreró 47 | tel. 971 65 52 25 | www.restaurantsaldecoco.com | Moderate–Expensive*). The young owner uses salt flakes from the rocky coast in her dishes, many of which feature freshly-caught fish from the waters of the Cabrera national park.

04:00pm After lunch, **drive back towards the Salines d'Es Trenc**. The white mountains of salt and the pink/blue grey evaporation pools lie just before the completely unspoilt beach of ⑬ **Es Trenc** → p. 89, which has been saved through the efforts of a GOB environmental initiative. Relax for the rest of the day between the dunes reminiscent of the North Sea islands and the turquoise coloured waters of the crescent-shaped bay. As evening approaches, you'll come to appreciate why the bay bears its name because the crowds disappear. On the way back, drive through Campos → p. 86, Porreres → p. 102 and Montuïri → p. 101 to return to ❶ **Sineu**.

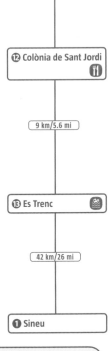

⑫ Colònia de Sant Jordi

9 km/5.6 mi

⑬ Es Trenc

42 km/26 mi

❶ Sineu

---

④ A HIKE TO THE HERMITAGE OF BETLEM

| START: ❶ Car park Ma3331 Artà–Betlem | ½ day |
| END: ❹ Colònia de Sant Pere | Walking time (without stops) 2½ hours |

| Distance: | Difficulty: |
| ⟹ 11 km/7 miles | .ıll easy |

WHAT TO PACK: sun protection, water, picnic lunch, swim gear, hiking boots, binoculars

IMPORTANT TIPS: the actual hike is only 7 km (4.3 miles) long; you will need a car for the other 4 km (2.5 miles). The hermitage does not have a restaurant or any residents. After walking back down, you can stop to eat in the small beach town of ❹ Colònia de Sant Pere.

This lovely hike to the hermitage of Betlem on the east coast offers a good dose of nature without being strenuous.

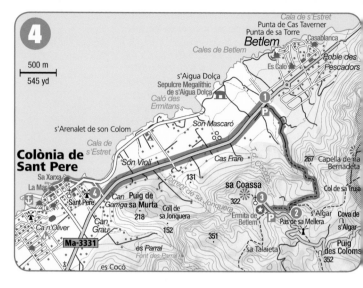

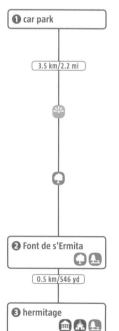

❶ car park

3.5 km/2.2 mi

❋

🔲

❷ Font de s'Ermita
🌳 🚰

0.5 km/546 yd

❸ hermitage
🏛 🏠 🚰

At **kilometre 7.5** on the **Ma3331 country road**, which runs from Artà to Betlem, you will find a ❶ car park next to a broad path. The signs from there will direct you to the "Cases de Betlem, Ermita de Betlem, S'Alqueria Vella". The trail heads **past abandoned buildings** and through the thorny brush right into the mountains.

The start of the path is sunny and steep. After just a few metres, you can enjoy the view of the bay of Alcúdia → p. 60. Then the trail becomes a bit more strenuous – and more interesting. It curves upwards, **following the course of a babbling mountain stream**. In spring, the bees buzz between gorse and rosemary bushes while the birds chirp loudly in the trees. The peninsula of the natural conservation area called the **Parc de Llevant** is uninhabited and largely unspoilt. Later on, the trail crosses **through a valley basin** overshadowed by spectacular rocky crags. Then you will finally come to the pass, where it's an easy walk as you pass a spring, the ❷ **Font de s'Ermita**, and grotto dedicated to the Virgin Mary. Sit down and rest for a few minutes on the benches and splash yourself with the water that bubbles over the little rocky canals.

It only take a few minutes to get to the ❸ **hermitage** → p. 66 from here. It sits in a high, fertile valley that has been farmed since the Moors occupied the island. There used to be more than 30 farmhouses here. In 1805, monks established the hermitage and gave it the biblical name of Betlem, i.e. Bethlehem. Up until a few years ago, hermits still lived here and cared for the fruit orchards and vegetable gardens. Today, the house is uninhabited, but the monks in the nearby town of Artà → p. 64 run the estate. Sheep and donkeys graze on the meadows that are filled with daisies in the spring. Light floods through the impressive church whose colourful rosette windows are worth a look. Enjoy the absolute silence inside the church. It's easy to while away the time in the open valley surrounding the hermitage. Kids can play, you can take a nap on the grass or grab your binoculars and look for goats on the cliffs of the mountains or eagles flying overhead. When you've had your fill, **hike back downhill to** the **car park**.

6 km / 3.7 mi

Before heading home, drive into ❹ **Colònia de Sant Pere** → **p. 70** and take advantage of the lovely INSIDER TIP **sandy beach** for a late afternoon swim. Afterwards, treat yourself to a nice meal in one of the restaurants in this small, peaceful resort town such as **Sa Xarxa**, which sits right next to the sea under tamarind trees.

❹ Colònia de Sant Pere

The Ermita de Betlem is the place to go for some peace and quiet

SPORTS & ACTIVITIES

Once the thermometer hits the 40-degree mark, many holidaymakers feel the only way to go is down to the sea. No wonder watersports such as swimming, diving, sailing and windsurfing is much in demand.

But the Mediterranean climate fosters ideal conditions for active sport holidays all year round be it on your bike, on foot in the mountains, or relaxing in the spa.

CANYONING

Canyoning is one of Mallorca's best kept secrets. Commercial tour operators such as *Món d'Aventura (tel. 9 71 53 52 48 | www.mondaventura.com)* and *Experience Mallorca (mobile tel. 6 87 35 89 22 | www.experience-mallorca.com)* have be-

gun to lead groups through the mountains on the west and north coast that are up to 1500 m/4920 ft high and crossed by many small streams. These torrents, called *torrents* or *barrancs,* have carved deep grooves into the calciferous rocks and offer themselves to climbing tours of various levels of difficulty. In the winter, the gorges are often full of water, cascades and churnholes, in the summer, they are dry and cool. Since most of the time you climb from the top down, children don't need that much strength, but they should be dexterouos and up for an adventure. They are roped up all the time and are accompanied by experienced climbers. A helmet is mandatory. All gear is provided; in the winter, this includes wetsuits.

Saddle up, dive in, lift off: Mallorca offers far more than lazy beach life; the island is ideal for a fitness holiday too

COASTEERING

The best outdoor activity of the summer! Roped up, with a helmet and a guide, you climb along the steep cliffs on the coast. Don't worry, there's little risk of injury. If your hand is wide off the mark, you just take a refreshing plunge into the sea beneath you. Still, you should have a head for heights and like sports. *Món d'Aventura (tel. 9 71 53 52 48 | www.mon daventura.com | from 40 euros)* and *Es-cull Aventura (mobile tel. 6 91 23 02 91 |* *www.escullaventura.com | from 55 euros incl. hotel transfer)* offer half-day tours, both are based in Pollença.

CYCLING

In spring and autumn, hobby and professional cyclists can be found on the island in their thousands. In a bid to promote sustainable tourism in the off seasons, the island government constantly extends the network of cycle paths and is working on an app showing suitable

A ride on the beach: the dream of many horse lovers comes true here

routes: in the flat area between Campanet and Campos for those wanting to take it easy, over the pass roads in the Tramuntana for real pros. Bike hire (also professional racing bikes) is available in all resorts from 9 euros per day. Cycling routes on *www.ciclismoenmallorca.com*.

DIVING

Mallorca's underwater world is especially lively along the rocky parts of the coast and off the Dragonera and Cabrera archipelagos. The water is clearest between April and June. The *Mallorca Diving* association *(www.mallorcadiving.com)* runs ten diving schools all over the island. A PADI beginner's certificate *(Scuba Diver)* takes two to three days and costs from 380 euros. Divers can book diving gear and a buddy for 100 euros.

In Calvià, you can dive without training: *Peter Diving (C/ Punta Negra 12 | tel. 9 71 75 20 26 | 45 min. from 60 eu-*

ros) is a cross between snorkelling and scuba diving; the oxygen comes out of a tank that's floating on the surface of the water. After a short introduction, you can dive right in without needing a certificate.

GOLF

Boasting 24 playable courses, Mallorca has turned itself into a new European golfing mecca these days. Save a lot on money on your golfing holiday with the *Mallorca Golfcard* for 119 euros *(www.mallorca-golfcard.com)*.

HIKING

Hiking on Mallorca – that's first and foremost the long-distance trail GR-221 leading through the Tramuntana mountains on the west coast in several stages. The *Ruta de Pedra en Sec (drywall trail)* runs along more than 150 km/93 miles between Andratx and Port de Pollença. It leads through an ancient cultivated landscape with terraced fields and mountain farms, oaks, pines and wild olive trees. The sea view is what makes this hiking experience unforgettable. You can find accomodation in seven *refugis,* serviced huts in Esporles, Deià, Sóller, Alaró, Lloseta, Escorca and Pollença *(overnight stay incl. breakfast from 11 euros, extra fee for dinner).* Be sure to book early! The island council has put together 14 easy, fun INSIDER TIP tours for families, which you can downlad in English here: *www.conselldemallorca.net/?&id_parent=491&id_section=3198&id_son=4004.*

HORSERIDING

The *Ranchos* or *Clubs Hípic* are set up in nearly every tourist centre. As the island is almost entirely in private hands and has many fences, it is best to join a guided hack. *Son Menut* horse riding centre *(Camí de Son Negre | www.sonmenut.com | day hack 113 euros, 1 hr 20 euros)* in Felanitx hires out Andalusian stallions to experienced riders. At the finca-turned-sports-hotel *Predio Son Serra* in Can Picafort all the action revolves around horseriding weeks and classes.

KITESURFING & WINDSURFING

On Mallorca, kitesurfing is only allowed in the bay of Pollença where you can find the *Kite Mallorca* school *(mobile tel. 6 47 89 11 22 | www.kitemallorca.com | three-day course 300 euros).* Windsurfers get their money's worth in the open bays of Alcúdia, Son Serra de Marina or Sa Rápita. Courses are offered by, among others: *Wind & Friends Watersports* (see p. 63) in Alcúdia or *Mallorca Adventure Sports (mobile tel. 6 29 47 22 68 |* *www.mallorcaadventuresports.com | 2 hrs 50 euros)* in Pollença, Portals Nous and Can Pastilla.

SAILING

There are 24 marinas along Mallorca's 550-km/342-mile long stretch of varied coastline where you can book sailing courses, pass your captain's exam or charter a boat, e.g. at *Charter del Mar (www.charterdelmar.com | 1 week from 1750 euros)* in Palma or *CM Charter Mallorca (www.cmcharter.de | 1 week from 2600 euros)* in Pollença.

WELLBEING

Over the last few years, Mallorca has become a proper spa holiday island. Recommendable facilities include the *Fontsanta Hotel (Ctra Campos–Colonia de San Jordi km 8.2 | Campos | tel. 9 71 65 50 16 | www.fontsantahotel.com | Moderate).* Three nights incl. spa treatments cost from 190 euros. The *Ayurveda Vedamar (mobile tel. 6 10 42 88 56 | www.vedamar.de)* at the *Hotel Sa Bassa Rotja (Cami de Sa Pedrera | Finca Son Orell | tel. 9 71 16 82 25 | www.sabassarotja.com | Moderate)* near Porreres offers Ayurveda retreats (relax day for 140 euros). The *Valparaíso Palace (C/ Francisco Vidal Sureda 23 | tel. 9 71 40 03 00 | www.grupotelvalparaiso.com | Expensive)* in Palma has the most extensive array of spa features (Kneipp pools, ice bridges, Asian treatments, pools and aroma baths). Non-hotel guests are also welcome in the spa. Five hours without treatments cost from 35 euros. An overview of the variety of spa services on the island can be found on the website of the specialist travel agency *Spa in Spain (C/ Son Rafalet 44b | Alaró | mobile tel. 6 28 14 96 40 | www.spa-in-spain.com).*

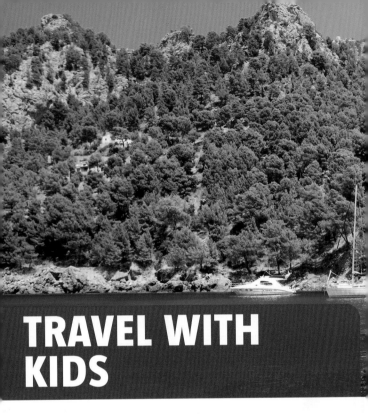

TRAVEL WITH KIDS

Spain is a very child-friendly country. Most locals are happy to satisfy kids' extra wishes, and they are tolerant if things happen to get a little noisy.

Flat sandy beaches and small coves, a back country with over a dozen leisure and nature parks, countless sports facilities and a well-maintained network of roads for trips by hire car make Mallorca one of the top destinations for family holidays in the Mediterranean. Beside the touristy stuff, there are a lot of places where you and your children can enjoy the island's wonderful nature, often even without an any fees. Add to this child-friendly menus in restaurants, excellent medical care and a range of goods virtually indistinguishable from the ones back home.

⭐ *Fishing boat tours,* which are available all around the island, make a very special and exciting family outing. You have to get yourself out of bed when it's still dark outside, but rising this early is well worth it: Once you've overcome your initial lazyness, you'll have a fantastic day out on the water with the local fishermen. Your tour starts with the sunrise over the sea and ends with freshly caught fish on your plate. In between, all passengers are allowed to help with the fishing, and probably, some dolphins will flap their fins here and there. *Pescaturisme Mallorca (www.pescaturis momallorca.com)* can match you with 40 fishermen everywhere on Mallorca all year; prices for a tour start from 65 euros.

Collecting seashells or an adrenaline rush: watery fun and exciting destinations for parents with children of all ages

PALMA & SURROUNDS

JUNGLE PARC JUNIOR
(151 E5) (*ØJ E8*)

This branch of *Jungle Parc* (see p. 52) in Bendinat offers six easy tours especially for kids between 4 and 11 years of age. *C/ Arquitecto Frances Casas | www.jungleparcjunior.es | April–Aug Fri–Wed 10am–5pm, Sept–March Sat/Sun 10am–5pm | admission 14 euros*

PALMA AQUARIUM ●
(156 C3) (*ØJ G8*)

This complex shelters 55 fish tanks with an impressive plant life and 8000 specimens from the world's oceans, a jungle landscape, a Mediterranean garden, restaurant and café. The transparent tunnel lets you get really close to the fish – and the sharks too... *Platja de Palma | motorway exit no. 10 (at Balneario 14, signposted) | www.palmaaquarium.com | daily 9:30am–6:30pm | adults 24 euros, children 14 euros*

PALMA JUMP (151 E4) (*W F7*)
Bouncy castles are for amateurs! Palma Jump on the outskirts of Palma boasts a whopping 50 trampolines, elastic basketball courts, climbing towers with airbags, slacklines and lots more. Children over 5 years are allowed to jump unaccompanied, younger kids can jump on the family trampoline with an adult during the week. There are also "jumping partys" for young people on Friday nights, with DJs and disco lights. *C/ Textil 3 | estate 33 | Son Valentí business park | www.palmajump.com | Sun–Thu 9am–10pm, Fri/Sat 9am–midnight | 10 euros/hour, family ticket (toddler and adult) 5 euros, jumping party (2 hours) 12 euros*

THE WEST

KATMANDU PARK (151 D5) (*W D8*)
An adventure park for kids following an American model. The scary, but beautifuzl main attraction is the house of Katmandu, a colourfully painted house in the Tibetan style, which stands on its head, and is haunted, but not only that. Eight darkened rooms full of surprises use acoustic and optical stimuli to take visitors from the torture chamber to the Yeti. The short films in the 5D cinemas are not for the faint-hearted. Also climbing adventures. *Av. Pedro Vaquer Ramis 9 | near the Magaluf Park Hotel | Magaluf | www.katmandupark.com | in the summer daily 10am–10pm | multi-day pass (all attractions once) adults 27.90 euros, children 21.90 euros, all-day pass adults 31.90 euros, children 25.90 euros*

PARC AVENTUR PUIGPUNYENT
(150 C–D3) (*W D6–7*)
The adventure and climbing park in the *Reserva Puig de Galatzó (5 km/3.1 miles from Puigpunyent, signposted | www.lareservamallorca.com | Nov–mid-Dec,* mid-Jan–March Sat/Sun, April–Oct daily 10am–6pm, last admission 4pm) features wobbly rope bridges, daring scrambles, great slides and darts. *Admission Reserva adults 14 euros, children 7 euros, flying foxes, mountain climbing, rope bridges an additional 14 euros each or 28 euros as a package*

WAVE HOUSE MALLORCA
(151 D5) (*W D8*)
Anyone over 1.07 m/3.51 ft tall can ride artificial waves up to 3 m/9.8 ft high at the Wave House. DJs, a skate track, cocktail bars and deckchairs make this a rather cool entertainment complex. Visitors have to show an ID, minors must be accompanied by an adult. *Av. Magaluf 18 | Magaluf | www.wavehousemallorca.com | May–Oct Mon–Thu 11am–7pm, Fri–Sun 10am–9pm | from 35 euros per hour*

THE NORTH

HIDROPARK (149 D3) (*W M3*)
The tame Mediterranean sea is too boring? At the Hidropark in Port d'Alcúdia, your kids can get their adrenaline rush. There are slides, wild water pools, chill-out zones, food stalls and paddling pools. *Av. Tucà | www.hidroparkalcudia.com | May–June, Sept–Oct daily 10am–5pm, July–Aug 10am–6pm | adults 22.90 euros, children over 3 years 16.60 euros*

KARTING CAN PICAFORT
(154 B1) (*W M4*)
On the kart track, children from four years of age can drive themselves or race over the tarmac in a double-seater with their parents. *Ctra. Alcudia–Artá s/n | Santa Margarita | www.kartingcanpicafort.com | May–Oct daily 10am–10pm, Nov–April Tue–Sun 9am–1pm, 3pm–7pm | 10 min. from 15 euros*

OBSERVATORIO DE BUITRES
(148 B4) (*K4*)

Meet Mallorca's emblematic animal in person: the black vulture! These imposing scavengers with a wingspan of up to 3 m/9.8 ft are normally circling high above the Tramuntana mountains. Only here, at the Finca Son Pons in the forest, can you get this close to them. Animals that are injured or unable to fly are taken care of here by the *Voltor Negre* foundation. You can watch feedings; there's also a film and information on the vultures and their habitat. *Motorway Palma–Alcúdia, exit 35 | www.fvsm.eu | Mon/Fri/1st Sat of the month June–Aug 9am–1pm, Sept–May 10am–2pm | admission free*

THE SOUTH

ARTESTRUZ (158 A4) (*K10*)

On this ostrich farm near Campos, you can get up close with these strange birds: You can observe ostrich babies, and if you are feeling courageous, you can feed the grown animals. You can buy many ostrich souvenirs at the shop and fresh ostrich eggs for the family omelette at home. *Ctra. Llucmajor–Ses Salines, km 40 | www.artestruzmallorca.com | daily 10am–5pm | adults 12 euros, children 4–12 years 7 euros*

COLLECTING FLOTSAM

A lot of stuff gets washed up on Mallorca's flat south coast – not only plastic, but also natural debris such as white, longish squid cuttlebones, seashells or felt balls: a lot of ideal materials for making mobiles! The balls, by the way, stem from the magic Possidonia plant that keeps the water clean and the sea animals thriving. There are also a great many seashells to be found in the bay of Palma near Portitxol (e.g. near the wind rose, Carrer Josep Amengual).

Parents beware: after your Mallorca holiday, the playground at home will seem rather bland

FESTIVALS & EVENTS

Festes and *firas*, festivals and fairs, are held throughout the year. In the summer, many communities celebrate their patron saints for one two two weeks with events ranging from the folk dance *ball de bot* to rock concerts. Because of the heat, many night markets have been established by now. Dive into the crowd at such a INSIDERTIP *fira nocturna* to buy crafts and bric-a-brac or to try local specialities. zu shoppen oder lokale Spezialitäten zu probieren. Get an overview at *mallorcamarketsandfestivals.com*.

FESTIVALS & EVENTS

JANUARY
16 Jan, *Eve of Sant Antoni:* spectacle in Sa Pobla, where *dimonis* (devils) roam the streets, dotted with burning *fogerós* (pyres)
from 20 Jan, *Sant Sebastià:* a week of festivities in Palma; on the eve of the day: live music with barbecues on all major squares and giant fireworks above the port

FEBRUARY
On the 1st Sun, *almond blossom festival* in Son Servera with various almond products and ● blooming trees all around

MARCH/APRIL
The *Day of the Balearic islands* on March 1st is celebrated in the capital with a medieval market at the harbour.
In the second March week, *Fira de Fang (pottery fair)* in Marratxí
Semana Santa/Pasqua: At 7pm on Maundy Thursday the biggest procession of masked fraternities starts in Palma. On Good Friday, for *Devallament*, confraternities from Pollença carry a statue of Christ down Calvary into the church.
In mid-April, the *World Folklore Festival*, every two years with processions and shows on Palma's squares
Mallorca's organic farmers's association organises the ⓥ *organic fair* in Porreres on the 3rd Sun in April.

MAY
From 2nd Sunday *Fira* in Sóller; Monday afternoon *moros i cristians:* The battle between Moors and Christians that took place in 1561 is recreated.
On the 2nd weekend, *medieval market* with artisans, music and food around the castle in Capdepera
Corpus Christi: two beautifully decked-out girls in eagle costumes take the lead at the INSIDERTIP *Processó de les Aguiles* procession in Pollença.

JUNE

Early June: ***International Jazz Festival*** in Cala d'Or

On the 2nd Sunday: ***Apricot fair*** in Porreres

On the 2nd weekend: ***Herb fair*** in Selva

23 June: ***Nit de Foc*** on Playa de Palma with candles, fireworks and dances

Highly original contest at the end of June in Son Servera on the Plaça Sant Joan: ***Nit del Cant de Gall****,* the night of the crowing roosters

JULY/AUGUST

On the 1st July weekend, ***Octopus Gastronomic Fair*** in Portocolom

16 July: a ***procession of ships*** sails through Port d'Andratx in the evening in honour of the Virgen del Carmen.

Music festivals in Valldemossa (Chopin), at Bellver Castle in Palma (Summer Serenades), in Deià/Son Marroig (chamber music) and in the Santo Domingo monastery in Pollença (featuring soloists of world renown); for exact dates, check the island's English-language press.

2 Aug: the battle between ***moros i cristians*** as the culmination of the ***festival of the patron saint of Pollença*** (7pm on the Rooster Fountain) seems impressively realistic.

OCTOBER/NOVEMBER

The largest autumn market is the ***Dijous Bo*** in mid-November in Inca. The first wine is celebrated in Binissalem, the largest melon in Vilafranca, the island's honey on the INSIDER TIP ***beekeeping fair*** in Llubí and the best sobrassada in Campos.

NATIONAL HOLIDAYS

1 Jan	New Year's Day
6 Jan	Epiphany
1 March	*Dia de les Illes Balears* (Balearic regional holiday)
29/30/ March/2 April 2018, 18/19/ 22 April 2019	Easter
1 May	Labour Day
25 July	*Fiesta Sant Jaume*
15 Aug	Assumption
12 Oct	*Dia de l'Hispanitat* (Discovery of America Day)
1 Nov	All Saints Day
6 Dec	*Dia de la Constitució* (Constitution Day)
8 Dec	Immaculate Conception
25/26 Dec	Christmas

LINKS, BLOGS, APPS & MORE

www.gotomallorca.net A virtual island guide with 360-degree panoramic images of sightseeing highlights such as the Banys Arabs in Palma and the castle of Capdepera as well as clubs, restaurants and beaches.

www.seemallorca.com Everything you need to know about travelling to Mallorca – beaches, events, activities, nightlife... even properties to buy

www.bestmallorcawalks.co.uk Does what it says on the tin! This site provides comprehensive information on a selection of tried and tested hiking trails in all parts of the island, safety precautions, links and much more

obcn.wordpress.com/tag/flor-de-sal-des-trenc/ Fine photos of various subjects by Santanyí-based photographer Oliver Brenneisen, amongst them the Flor de Sal salt extraction in Ses Salines

www.digamemallorca.com Up-to-date guide to cultural, gastronomic and touristic events from Mallorca's acclaimed listings magazine

walkingonwords.com/en This website (and app) invites you to take literary tours across the island. Explore the sites of novels and the living quarters of writers on a hike or a car tour

www.platgesdebalears.com Descriptions of all the beaches on Mallorca and the neighbouring islands. The multilingual website is sponsored by the Balearic government

en.balearsnatura.com The Spanish Ministry of Agriculture, Food and the Environment provides information about all the nature preserve areas on the Balearic Islands in English

www.anna-nicholas.com British writer Anna Nicholas describes her expat life on Mallorca – as she has also done in several books

Regardless of whether you are still preparing your trip or already on Mallorca: these addresses will provide you with more information, videos and networks to make your holiday even more enjoyable.

www.farsdebalears.org Tour guide featuring Mallorca's 16 lighthouses. The animated, 360-degree panoramic feature enables you to enjoy the view already from your sofa and explore the interiors. Great pictures of land and sea

www.youtube.com/watch?v= Khd Naxwnpzg A declaration of love on video: Javier Pierotti's "I love Mallorca" offers beautiful images of the island accompanied by equally beautiful music

www.youtube.com/watch?v= K6d8aqJYVtc Mallorca's anthem "La Balanguera", sung with gusto by the Mallorcan chanson singer Maria del Mar Bonet (4 mins 31 sec)

www.youtube.com/watch?v= wjnpsYYWxKE Every year at the end of September, the residents of the village of Bunyola run through the streets in their underwear. Men and women, young and old, strip down in honour of the patron Sant Mateu

www.produccionsblau.com The Blau record label has been producing works by Balearic musicians for many years. On their website you can listen in

VIDEOS & MUSIC

Transport Mallorca This unfortunately rather confusing free app for iOS and android offers up-to-date timetables for city and regional buses, subways and trains

Arbolapp Super tree identification app for the Balearic Islands. Unfortunately, it is only available in Spanish, but it is free and has good illustrations; for iOS and android

Mallorca Rutes: Palma free iOS guide through Palma's Old Town. 40 points of interest with contact information plus restaurants and shops

APPS

TRAVEL TIPS

ARRIVAL

Driving to Mallorca from London involves about 1100 km (684 miles) of motorway driving, via Orleans – Bourges – Clermond-Ferrand – Millau to Barcelona. Toll charges in France and Spain: about 100 euros.

Travel time from London to Barcelona on sleeper or daytime trains is about 15 hours. Depending on the season, a regular second-class return ticket from London starts from around 260 euros. *www.seat61.com* is an excellent site for timetables and ticketing links. Keep an eye out for special offers!

International flights touch down at Palma de Mallorca (Son Sant Joan) airport). Flight time from London is under 2.5 hours, and Palma is served by most UK regional airports. The majority of holidaymakers uses the charter flight offers (expect to pay between 100 and 300 euros). Economy-class scheduled flights with BA or Iberia range between 200 and 500 euros. The cheapest option (starting at 40 euros) are seasonal special offers, as well as booking well in advance. Several hire-car firms tout for business at the airport; taxis offer transfers to the island's other regions and towns. The longest trip, to Cala Rajada, costs about 90 euros, to Palma around 25 euros. Normal-scheduled buses travel from the airport to Palma (5 euros) and as of 2017 to many coastal resorts as well (*www.tib.org*, 5–12 euros).

The shipping companies *Baleària (www.balearia.com)* and *Acciona Trasmediterránea (www.trasmediterranea. com)* connect Mallorca to the mainland ports Barcelona, Valencia and Dénia. The 7-hour crossing (car and two adults return) costs around 500 euros. Specialised travel agencies are *www.aferry.com, www. ocean24.de* and *www.directferries.com*.

RESPONSIBLE TRAVEL

It doesn't take a lot to be environmentally friendly whilst travelling. Don't just think about your carbon footprint whilst flying to and from your holiday destination but also about how you can protect nature and culture abroad. As a tourist it is especially important to respect nature, look out for local products, cycle instead of driving, save water and much more. If you would like to find out more about eco-tourism please visit: *www.ecotourism.org*

BANKS & MONEY

Practically all towns on the island have several banks, and there are few places without an ATM cash machine.

BUSES & TRAINS

The underground bus and railway station in Palma, below the park opposite Plaça Espanya, is called Estació Intermodal. This is where the trains to/from Inca–Muro–Sa Pobla or Inca–Sineu–Monacor and all overland buses to/from all towns on the island leave from. There is an information point with English-speaking staff. The Balearic regional transport authority *TIB (tel. 9 71 17 77 77 | www.tib. org)* provides information in multiple languages on its website and by telephone about connections, timetables and prices. The multi-ride tickets mostly only save money if you travel the exact same route several times (i.e. for commuters). Tickets can be bought from the driver. The railway station also houses a bike hire facility – apart from the historic quarter and in the entirely pedestrianised areas, a bike is not a bad way to get around Palma, and green to boot! Opposite the railway hotel you will find the Art Nouveau railway station serving the nostalgic *Ferrocarril de Sóller.* There are precious few connections between the towns on the island; everything centres around Palma.

CAMPSITES

Wild camping outside a campground is forbidden, but if you call ahead, you can pitch your tent at the *Lluc Monastery (300 spaces | showers, drinking water)* or in the *Es Pixarells* compound *(30 spaces | toilet, drinking water | Ctra. Lluc–Escorca).* Both campsites are open throughout the year. Reservations at *tel. 9 71 51 70 70.* The campsite *S'Arenalet (30 spaces | toilets, showers, drinking water | Ctra. Artà–Cala Torta | tel. 9 71 17 76 52 | refugis@ibanat. caib.es | closed Jan)* is beautifully located on the unspoilt coast of Artà. Individual hikers can call the league for the protection of birds, *GOB (C/ Manuel Sanchis Guarner 10 | Palma | tel. 9 71 49 60 60)* and camp out in their compound, ☙ *La Trapa (Andratx | can only be reached on foot | 4 spaces | all year),* located in the mountains with a great view of the sea and the island of Dragonera. The *Hipocam-*

po grounds *(C/ Es Domingos Vells | Cales de Mallorca | tel. 9 71 83 37 15 | www.club-hipocampo.com)* are located on the east coast. They offer a large refuge for groups and spaces for tents. Book ahead!

CAR HIRE

During peak season, hundreds of car-hire companies offer around 60,000 rental

BUDGETING

Taxi	0.88 euros *per kilometre*
Coffee	from 1.20 euros *for an espresso*
Beach	about 12–15 euros *for two recliners with parasol*
Tapas	from 3.50 euros *for a small portion*
Ice cream	from 1.50 euros *for a scoop*
Bike hire	from 10 euros *per day*

cars. Check and contrast the terms: particularly cheap offers aren't necessarily the most trustworthy. It is worth taking out fully comprehensive insurance with no excess in case of damage. A hire car of the lower category costs about 175 euros a week excluding petrol – when you book from home that is. Generally hire cars booked over the internet from home (from and to the airport) are a lot cheaper than those rented on a whim in holiday centres.

CLIMATE, WHEN TO GO

The north is cooler than the south. Spring is usually mild with cool evenings and rain showers. Summers are hot with occasional thunder and lightning, August has high levels of humidity. Autumn stays warm well into October, after that the first cold spells arrive, and with them a lot of precipitation. Winters are predominantly mild, and due to high humidity in the evening and at night turn cool to cold.

CONSULATES AND EMBASSIES

BRITISH CONSULATE
C/ Convent dels Caputxins | 4 Edificio Orisba B 4º | Palma | tel. 93 366 6200 | ukinspain.fco.gov.uk/en

IRISH CONSULATE GENERAL
San Miguel, 68 | Palma | tel. 971 719 244

US CONSULATE AGENCY
Porto Pi, 8 | Palma | tel. 971 40 37 07

CUSTOMS

EU citizens can import and export goods for their personal use tax-free (800 cigarettes, 1 kg tobacco, 90 l of wine, 10 l of spirits over 22 %).
Visitors from other countries must observe the following limits, except for items for personal use. Duty free are: max. 50 g perfume, 200 cigarettes, 50 cigars, 250 g tobacco, 1 L of spirits (over 22 % vol.), 2 L of spirits (under 22 % vol.), 2 L of any wine.

DRIVING

Apart from driving on the right-hand side of the road, traffic regulations are broadly similar to the UK. Maximum speed limits on motorways: 120 km/h (75 mph); on country roads: 90 km/h (55 mph). Seat belts have to be worn at all times; and a helmet must be worn on all motorised two-wheel vehicles. Blood alcohol limit: 0.5. Carrying a fluorescent vest is compulsory, and using a mobile phone whilst driving is prohibited. Penalties *(multas)* are very high (sometimes more than 100 euros!). If you pay your fine right away or within a few days, you'll receive a discount of up to 50 per cent depending on the municipality. In villages and towns, blue lines pinpoint limited and payable parking, yellow ones signal no parking. Ignore parking restrictions at your peril unless you want to pay *multas* or have your car towed away. In the blue parking zones in the centre of Palma, you have to get a pay and display ticket at the machine for 120 to 180 minutes. If you exceed that time, you risk a wheel clamp or will even be towed away. You'll have unlimited parking time in the expensive multistorey car parks of the capital, but you should get there early in the morning – later on, Palma, the city with the highest traffic density in Spain, will be jam-packed.

ECO TOURISM TAX

As of 1st July 2016, visitors to Mallorca have to pay a visitor's tax, the Ecotasa, the earnings of which are supposed to promote sustainable tourism. It is payable by every guest over 17 per overnight stay. Tourists arriving on Mallorca on a cruiseship have to pay as well. In peak season (from May to October) you'll have to pay between 0.50 and 2 euros per day plus VAT, depending on the category of your accomodation. In the low season, it's half that amount. If you stay ten days or longer, you'll get a reduction. The tax is collected at the hotel's reception desk or by the landlord of your finca or holiday flat.

ry a valid passport. All children must travel with their own passport.

EMERGENCY

National emergency number (police, fire service, ambulance): *tel. 112*

FOREST FIRES

There isn't that much forest on Mallorca in the first place. Which is why forest fires, often occurring after extended periods of hot weather and drought, can have a dramatic impact. In 2016, there were 79 fires on the Balearic islands, 150 ha/370 acres of forest were destroyed. Alongside pyromaniacs and lightning striking, carelessness and negligence are the biggest factors. Don't ever throw a cigarette butt out of a driving car, don't leave any glass bottles lying around and don't start a barbecue in the forest – there are hefty fines!

HEALTH

The island has a comprehensive network of doctors' surgeries (you'll find addresses of English-speaking medics in the Majorca Daily Bulletin available from news stands) and pharmacies *(farmacias)*. There are also eleven private and ten state-run hospitals (providing interpreters). Over a dozen alternative medicine services have settled on Mallorca. The holiday resorts have their own *centros médicos,* and the Red Cross *(Cruz Roja)* provides first aid on many beaches. Medical emergencies (islandwide, around the clock) *Red Cross: tel. 9 71 20 22 22.*

IMMIGRATION

Holidaymakers from EU countries usually aren't checked anymore, but should car-

CURRENCY CONVERTER

£	€	€	£
1	1.09	1	0.92
3	3.28	3	2.75
5	5.46	5	4.58
13	14.20	13	11.90
40	43.70	40	36.63
75	82	75	68
120	130	120	110
250	273	250	229
500	546	500	458

$	€	€	$
1	0.84	1	1.19
3	1.69	3	3.56
5	4.22	5	5.93
13	11	13	15.42
40	34	40	47.44
75	63	75	89
120	101	120	142
250	211	250	296
500	422	500	593

For current exchange rates see www.xe.com

INFORMATION

SPANISH TOURIST OFFICE
www.spain.info
UK: 64 North Row | London W1K 7DE | tel. 020 7317 2011
US: Los Angeles, Miami, New York, Chicago
Canada: 2 Bloor Street West | Suite 3402 | Ontario M4W 3E2 | Toronto | tel. 4169614079

INTERNET & WIFI

Many cafés and restaurants now offer their customers free WiFi. Most bars share their network with the customers, if you ask for the password. Mallorca is working to establish Europe's largest wireless network; it already offers 300 WiFi Hotspots (mallorca-wifi). Places with unrestricted internet access in Palma include the Platja de Palma, the old jetty, the Parc de la Mar and the subterranean bus terminal on the Plaça Espanya, elsewhere, for example, the coast near Calvià and the beach at Port d'Alcúdia.

ISLAND HOPPING

If you want to explore one of the other Balearic islands from Mallorca, you should plan at least two days for the trip. From Palma, Iberia, Vueling and Air Europa fly to Menorca and Ibiza in approx. 20 minutes. The *Baleària* ferrys *(www. balearia.com)* depart either from Alcúdia and take you to Menorca in about 90 minutes, or from Palma, reaching Ibiza after about four hours. Formentera can only be reached by ferry from Ibiza. Apart from Baleària, *Acciona Trasmediterránea (www. trasmediterranea.es)* also goes there.

MARINAS

A list of all Balearic marinas, with information on location, size, number of moorings, maximum length of boats allowed and port facilities, as well as of all providers of charter yachts, can be obtained from *Mallorca nautic | Paseo Marítimo 16a | Palma | tel. 9 71 28 00 07 | www.mallorcanautic.com.* The only agency on the Balearics listing all charter companies (over 80) describes all available boat

WEATHER ON MALLORCA

	Jan	Feb	March	April	May	June	July	Aug	Sept	Oct	Nov	Dec
Daytime temperatures in °C/°F												
	14/57	15/59	17/63	19/66	23/73	27/81	29/84	30/86	27/81	23/73	18/64	15/59
Night time temperatures in °C/°F												
	6/43	6/43	7/45	9/48	13/55	16/61	19/66	19/66	18/64	14/57	10/50	7/45
☀	5	6	6	7	10	10	11	11	8	6	5	5
☂	6	6	6	4	4	2	1	2	5	6	7	7
〜	14/57	13/55	14/57	15/59	17/63	21/70	24/75	25/77	24/75	21/70	18/64	15/59

types on its website and can also arrange skippers for about 135 euros per day.

MEDIA

Nearly all hotels offer British and other English-language TV programmes via satellite. News stands sell British newspapers, as well as the English-language daily, weekly and monthly papers and magazines, such as Majorca Daily Bulletin, Dígame or Euro Weekly News. The English-language island radio *(www.radioonemallorca.com)* broadcasts 24/7 on 105.6 FM.

OPENING HOURS

Restaurants are usually open *1–4pm and 7:30–11pm*, shops on weekdays *9am–1/1:30pm, 4–8:30pm and longer.*

PHONE & MOBILE PHONE

Using the hotel telephone is very expensive. For calls outside Spain dial 00 followed by the dialling code for the country (UK 44, Ireland 353, US and Canada 1) and of the town/city (without the 0), then the number of the person you are calling. The code for Spain is 0034. Spanish telephone numbers consist of 9 digits and there are no local area codes. Mallorcan landlines begin with 971 or (rarely) 871 whilst mobile numbers begin with a 6 or (rarely) 7. The biggest providers of mobile phone services are Movistar, Orange and Vodafone.

POST

Stamps can be bought from the post office *(correos)* and in the tobacco shops *(tabaco, estanco)*. Letterboxes are yellow. Post stamped with private firms' stamps will only be collected from that particular company's letterbox!

PRICES

The prices on Mallorca are similar to those in the rest of Europe. The weekly markets are not bazaars and haggling over prices is uncommon. Fresh meat continues to be good value, but not fresh fish, as it has become rare here too. Tourists complain about high prices in restaurants – rightly so in many places, especially as prices often seem to bear little relation to the quality. A bottle of table wine costing some 2.50 euros in the supermarket can cost 15 times as much in a restaurant. Organised trips are also a drain on holiday finances: 30–65 euros for a day excursion without packed lunch or a show evening with a set menu.

TIPPING

Anybody working in the service industry is glad of a tip. In restaurants, it is customary to add up to 10 per cent to the total bill. Maids expect 5–6 euros per week. The charge for taxis or private coach transport should be rounded up generously, and guides usually receive a gratuity of around 5–10 euros or more if you were happy with the service.

WATER

Even after the construction of the desalination plants near Palma and the deployment of mobile desalination units, the potable water supply remains a problem, especially in years with little rain. In high summer the drinking water in many coastal areas becomes very salty. Also, the island consists of limestone, making the water very hard. The best thing to do is to drink only mineral water and restrict water use to essential needs.

USEFUL PHRASES CATALAN

PRONUNCIATION

c	like "s" before "e" and "i" (e.g. Barcelona); like "k" before "a", "o" and "u" (e.g. Casa)
ç	pronounced like "s" (e.g. França)
g	like "s" in "pleasure" before "e" and "i"; like "g" in "get" before "a", "o" and "u"
l·l	pronounced like "l"
que/qui	the "u" is always silent, so "qu" sounds like "k" (e.g. perquè)
v	at the start of a word and after consonants like "b" (e.g. València)
x	like "sh" (e.g. Xina)

IN BRIEF

Yes/No/Maybe	Sí/No/Potser
Please/Thank you/Sorry	Sisplau/Gràcies/ Perdoni
May I ...?	Puc ...?
Pardon?	Com diu *(Sie)*?/Com dius *(Du)*?
I would like to .../	Voldria.../
Have you got ...?	Té...?
How much is ...?	Quant val...?
I (don't) like this	(no) m'agrada
good	bo/bé *(Adverb)*
bad	dolent/malament *(Adverb)*
Help!/Attention!/Caution!	Ajuda!/Compte!/Cura!
ambulance	ambulància
police/fire brigade	policia/bombers
Prohibition/forbidden	prohibició/prohibit
danger/dangerous	perill/perillós
May I take a photo here/of you?	Puc fer-li una foto aquí?

GREETINGS, FAREWELL

Good morning!/afternoon!	Bon dia!
Good evening!/night!	Bona tarda!/Bona nit!
Hello!/Goodbye!	Hola!/Adéu! Passi-ho bé!
See you	Adéu!
My name is ...	Em dic...
What's your name?	Com es diu?
I come from...	Sóc de ...

Parles Català?

"Do you speak Catalan?" This guide will help you to say the basic words and phrases in Catalan.

DATE & TIME

Monday/Tuesday	dilluns/dimarts
Wednesday/Thursday	dimecres/dijous
Friday/Saturday	divendres/dissabte
Sunday/working day	diumenge/dia laborable
holiday	dia festiu
today/tomorrow/yesterday	avui/demà/ahir
hour/minute	hora/minut
day/night/week	dia/nit/setmana
It's three o'clock.	Són les tres.

TRAVEL

open/closed	obert/tancat
entrance/driveway	entrada
exit/exit	sortida
departure/arrival	sortida/arribada
toilets/restrooms / ladies/gentlemen	Lavabos/Dones/Homes
Where is ...?/Where are ...?	On està...?/On estan...?
left/right	a l'esquerra/a la dreta
close/far	a prop/lluny
bus	bus
taxi/cab	taxi
bus stop/cab stand	parada/parada de taxis
parking lot/parking garage	aparcament/garatge
street map/map	pla de la ciutat/mapa
train station/harbour	estació/port
airport	aeroport
schedule/ticket	horario/bitllet
train / platform/track	tren/via
platform	andana
I would like to rent ...	Voldria llogar...
a car/a bicycle	un cotxe/una bicicleta
petrol/gas station	gasolinera
petrol/gas / diesel	gasolina/gasoil
breakdown/repair shop	avaria/taller

FOOD & DRINK

Could you please book a table for tonight for four?	Voldriem reservar una taula per a quatre persones per avui al vespre

on the terrace	a la terrassa
The menu, please	la carta, sisplau
Could I please have ...?	Podria portar-me ...?
bottle/carafe/glass	ampolla/garrafa/got
salt/pepper/sugar	sal/pebrot/sucre
vinegar/oil	vinagre/oli
vegetarian/	vegetarià/vegetariana/
allergy	allèrgia
May I have the bill, please?	El compte, sisplau

SHOPPING

Where can I find...?	On hi ha...?
I'd like .../	voldria/
I'm looking for ...	estic buscant...
pharmacy/chemist	farmacia/drogueria
baker/market	forn/mercat
shopping center	centre comercial/gran magatzem
supermarket	supermercat
kiosk	quiosc
expensive/cheap/price	car/barat/preu
organically grown	de cultiu ecológic

ACCOMMODATION

I have booked a room	He reservat una habitació
Do you have any ... left?	Encara té...
single room	una habitació individual
double room	una habitació doble
breakfast/half board	esmorzar/mitja pensió
full board	pensió completa
at the front/seafront	exterior/amb vistes al mar
shower/sit down bath	dutxa/bany
balcony/terrace	balcó/terrassa

BANKS, MONEY & CREDIT CARDS

bank/ATM	banc/caixer automàtic
pin code	codi secret
cash/	al comptat/
credit card	amb targeta de crèdit
change	canvi

HEALTH

doctor/dentist/paediatrician	metge/dentista/pediatre
hospital/emergency clinic	hospital/urgència
fever/pain	febre/dolor
inflamed/injured	inflamat/ferit
plaster/bandage	tireta/embenat
ointment/cream	pomada/crema
pain reliever/tablet	analgèsic/pastilla

POST, TELECOMMUNICATIONS & MEDIA

stamp/letter/postcard	segell/carta/ postal
I need a landline phone card	Necessito una targeta telefònica per la xarxa fixa
I'm looking for a prepaid card for my mobile	Estic buscant una targeta de prepagament pel mòbil
Where can I find internet access?	On em puc connectar a Internet?
Do I need a special area code?	He de marcar algun prefix determinat?
socket/adapter/charger	endoll/adaptador/carregador
computer/battery/ rechargeable battery	ordinador/bateria/ acumulador
at sign (@)	arrova
internet address	adreça d'internet (URL)
e-mail address	adreça de correu electrònic
e-mail/file/print	correu electrònic/fitxer/imprimir

LEISURE, SPORTS & BEACH

beach	platja
sunshade/lounger	para-sol/gandula

NUMBERS

0 zero	12 dotze	60 seixanta
1 un/una	13 tretze	70 setanta
2 dos/dues	14 catorze	80 vuitanta
3 tres	15 quinze	90 noranta
4 quatre	16 setze	100 cent
5 cinc	17 disset	200 dos-cents/dues-centes
6 sis	18 divuit	1000 mil
7 set	19 dinou	2000 dos mil
8 vuit	20 vint	10000 deu mil
9 nou	30 trenta	
10 deu	40 quaranta	½ mig
11 onze	50 cinquanta	¼ un quart

ROAD ATLAS

The green line indicates the Discovery Tour "Mallorca at a glance"
The blue line indicates the other Discovery Tours

All tours are also marked on the pull-out map

Photo: Alcúdia Bay

Travelling around Mallorca

The map on the back cover shows how the area has been sub-divided

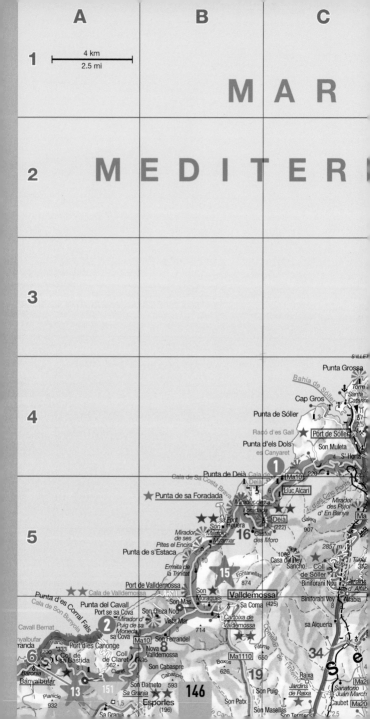

A B C

1
4 km
2.5 mi

M A R

2
M E D I T E R

3

S'ILLE

Punta Grossa

Bahía de Sóller

Torre
Santa
Catarina

Cap Gros

4
Punta de Sóller

Port de Sóller

Racó d'es Gall

Son Muleta

Punta d'els Dols

S' Horta

es Canyaret

Punta de Deià   Cala de

Cala de Sa Costa Brava

Ma10   226

Deià

Lluc Alcari

★ Punta de sa Foradada

Mirador de sa
Foradada

d' es Cinc Ports

Mirador
des Pujol
d' En Banya

Ma

★★   Sa Font
Son   Figuera
Mamba

Deià
(222)

Galera
907

5
Mirador
de ses
Pites el Encira

Miramar

16

Castell
des Moro

2857 m

Punta de s'Estaca

Mirador
de ses

106°   Casa del Rey
Sancho

Túnel
312

Ermita de
la Trinitat

Coll
de Sóller

290

Port de Valldemossa

Fontanellas
874

15

Biniforani Nou

Jardins
d' Alfab

★★ Cala de Valldemossa

Son
Moragues

Valldemossa

Biniforani Vey

Alfabia

Punta d'es Corral Fals

Cala de Son Bunyola

Punta del Cavall
Port se sa Cova

2

Mirador d' es
Puig de sa
Moneda
sa Cova

Son Oleza Nou

Sa Coma (425)

sa Alqueria

Vista Mar

Cala de
Claret

Son Ferrandel

Cartoixa de
Valldemossa

34

714

Cavall Bernat

Plana
333

290

Port d'es Canonge

Ma10

e

Coll
d' sa Bastida

Coll
de Claret   562

Nova
Valldemossa

8

Fatima

S

anda

6

Baronia

Son Cabaspre

Ma1110   650

Boxos
626

19

Son Puig

Jardins
de Raixa

Sanatorio
Juán March

Ma2

Banyalbufar

13   151

Son Dameto   593

Sa Granja ★★

Esporles
(196)

146

Raixa

Caubet   Ma20

Planície
932

Son Patx

Son Masellas

Sa Granja

e Can

2.5

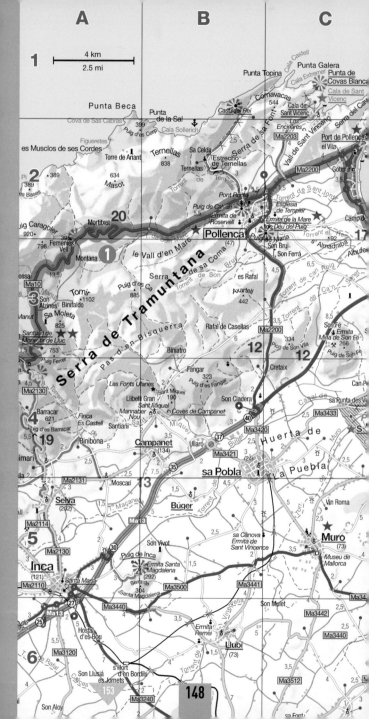

	A	B	C
1		MAR	
	MEDITERRÀNIA		

MAR

MEDITERRÀNIA

★ *Torre Talaia de Ses Anim...*
Punta d' es Verge

Punta de Son Serralta
Emp...

Cala Estellencs
Port de Estellencs
Cala Ca's Xeramier
Platja Can Pruaga   Coll d'es Pi
Punta de sa Lluenta   825.2   Estell...

★★ *Mirador de*
R. Roca   es Grau
Punta de sa Foradada   Serra d' es Pinotells   Galatzó
Cala de ses Ortigues   1026
Punta de sa Llova   Esclop
es Barraca   .926   ★
Descarregador   *La Reserva Parc Natural*   d
Punta d'en Fabiolet   Fondal de
ses Basses   Bachàs   Ma10
Morro Ratjada   491.   343
SA DRAGONERA   sa Trapa   S   e   r   r   Caserio Galatzó
Cala   Coll de   422   s'Alqueria   M
Basset   sa Gremola   Abidala   Grau   482 • Son Mortolá
Parc   Torre   Son Guiém   Son Boch   Son Cl
Natural   en Basset   330   5,5   8,5
Punta   **Sant Elm**   Son Castell   Ma1031   Es
Negra   Basset   s'Arracó   Sa Coma   Capdella
de Dragonera   3   (101)   • Son Mas   Ma1031
310   *I. Pantaleu*   Emita   Ma1030   **Andratx**   Son Alfonso
4 Cala Llebeitx   *Castell*   Enrich   Ma1   (133)   Son Vich Nou
Cap Llebeitx   *de Sant Elm*   318   Garras   461   Tora
Punta Galinda   Antió   D Coll   125   Son Fortuny
Cala d'Antió   276   d'Andritxol   Ma1   Tunel de
Cap Falcóns   Ma1   Son Vich   12
Punta Moragues   Port d'Andratx   125   840 m   Ma1012
Badia de Andratx   1.5   Son Vich   Peguera
Ma1020   Camp   de Mar   sa Romana
Can Inglés   Platja   Fornells   (20)
Cala Racó   de Camp   Cala   Platja   (18)
Cala Marmassen   de Mar   Fornells   de
Cap de sa Mola   Cala Llamp   Peguera   Costa de
Cap d' es Llamp   Cala Andritxol   Punta des Castellot   la Calma
Ensenada   Cala de Santa Ponça
de Santa Ponça   *sa Caleta*   Santa P
Na Foradada
I. de los CONEJOS   Son F
I. MALGRATS
Punta Enguisa
Cala de Penyes Rotjes   el Toro
4 km   Cala
2.5 mi   Refeubeitx
I. DEL TORO   d'

150

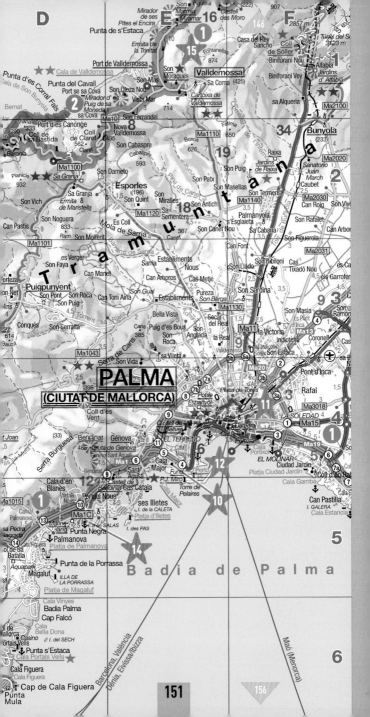

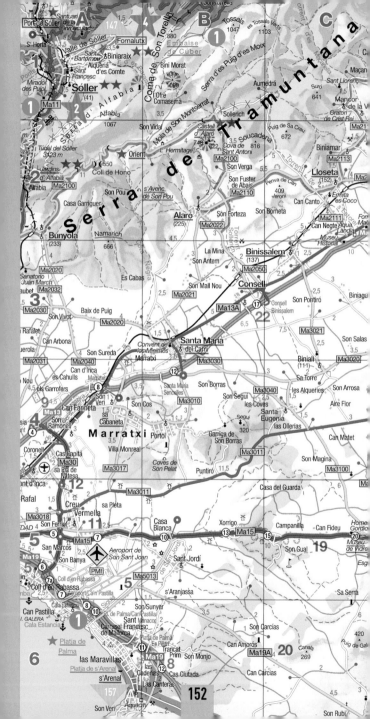

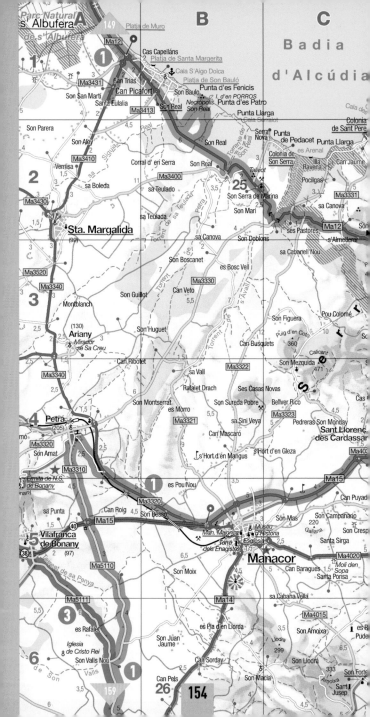

PALMA ★★
(CIUTAT DE MALLORCA)

Badia de Palma

MAR

MEDITERRÀNIA

4 km
2.5 mi

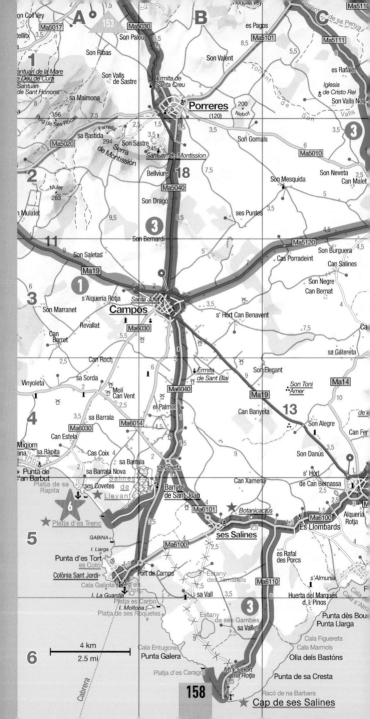

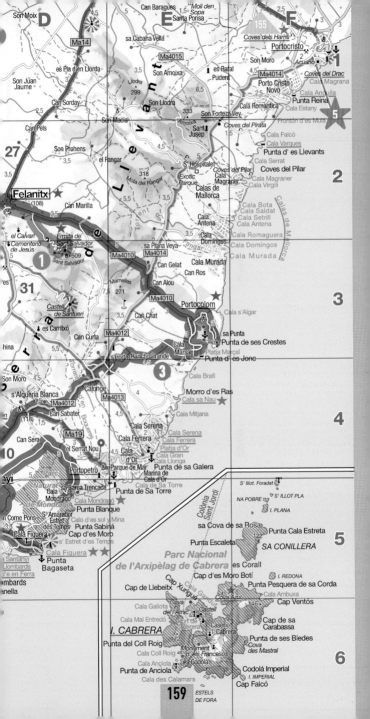

KEY TO ROAD ATLAS

German	Symbol	English
Autobahn · Gebührenpflichtige Anschlussstelle · Gebührenstelle · Anschlussstelle mit Nummer · Rasthaus mit Übernachtung · Raststätte · Kleinraststätte · Tankstelle · Parkplatz mit und ohne WC	Trento	Motorway · Toll junction · Toll station · Junction with number · Motel · Restaurant · Snackbar · Filling-station · Parking place with and without WC
Autobahn in Bau und geplant mit Datum der voraussichtlichen Verkehrsübergabe	Datum Date	Motorway under construction and projected with expected date of opening
Zweibahnige Straße (4-spurig)		Dual carriageway (4 lanes)
Fernverkehrsstraße · Straßennummern	14 E45	Trunk road · Road numbers
Wichtige Hauptstraße		Important main road
Hauptstraße · Tunnel · Brücke	)=(	Main road · Tunnel · Bridge
Nebenstraßen		Minor roads
Fahrweg · Fußweg		Track · Footpath
Wanderweg (Auswahl)		Tourist footpath (selection)
Eisenbahn mit Fernverkehr		Main line railway
Zahnradbahn, Standseilbahn		Rack-railway, funicular
Kabinenschwebebahn · Sessellift		Aerial cableway · Chair-lift
Autofähre · Personenfähre		Car ferry · Passenger ferry
Schifffahrtslinie		Shipping route
Naturschutzgebiet · Sperrgebiet		Nature reserve · Prohibited area
Nationalpark · Naturpark · Wald		National park · natural park · Forest
Straße für Kfz. gesperrt	X	Road closed to motor vehicles
Straße mit Gebühr		Toll road
Straße mit Wintersperre	XII-II	Road closed in winter
Straße für Wohnanhänger gesperrt bzw. nicht empfehlenswert		Road closed or not recommended for caravans
Touristenstraße · Pass	Weinstraße ⌃1510	Tourist route · Pass
Schöner Ausblick · Rundblick · Landschaftlich bes. schöne Strecke		Scenic view · Panoramic view · Route with beautiful scenery
Heilbad · Schwimmbad		Spa · Swimming pool
Jugendherberge · Campingplatz		Youth hostel · Camping site
Golfplatz · Sprungschanze		Golf-course · Ski jump
Kirche im Ort, freistehend · Kapelle		Church · Chapel
Kloster · Klosterruine		Monastery · Monastery ruin
Synagoge · Moschee		Synagogue · Mosque
Schloss, Burg · Schloss-, Burgruine		Palace, castle · Ruin
Turm · Funk-, Fernsehturm		Tower · Radio-, TV-tower
Leuchtturm · Kraftwerk		Lighthouse · Power station
Wasserfall · Schleuse		Waterfall · Lock
Bauwerk · Marktplatz, Areal		Important building · Market place, area
Ausgrabungs- u. Ruinenstätte · Bergwerk		Arch. excavation, ruins · Mine
Dolmen · Menhir · Nuraghen		Dolmen · Menhir · Nuraghe
Hünen-, Hügelgrab · Soldatenfriedhof		Cairn · Military cemetery
Hotel, Gasthaus, Berghütte · Höhle		Hotel, inn, refuge · Cave

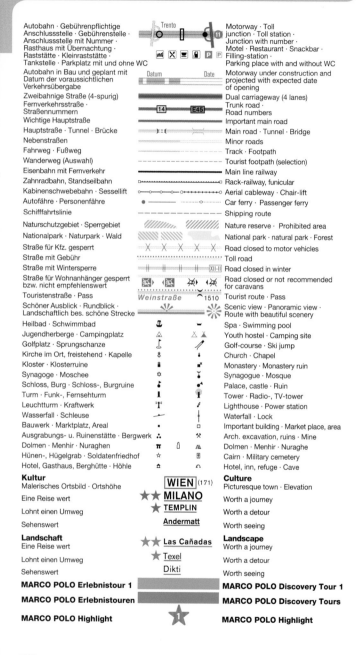

Kultur		Culture
Malerisches Ortsbild · Ortshöhe	WIEN (171)	Picturesque town · Elevation
Eine Reise wert	★★ MILANO	Worth a journey
Lohnt einen Umweg	★ TEMPLIN	Worth a detour
Sehenswert	Andermatt	Worth seeing

Landschaft		Landscape
Eine Reise wert	★★ Las Cañadas	Worth a journey
Lohnt einen Umweg	★ Texel	Worth a detour
Sehenswert	Dikti	Worth seeing

MARCO POLO Erlebnistour 1		MARCO POLO Discovery Tour 1
MARCO POLO Erlebnistouren		MARCO POLO Discovery Tours
MARCO POLO Highlight	★1	MARCO POLO Highlight

FOR YOUR NEXT TRIP...

MARCO POLO TRAVEL GUIDES

Algarve
Amsterdam
Andalucia
Athens
Australia
Austria
Bali & Lombok
Bangkok
Barcelona
Berlin
Brazil
Bruges
Brussels
Budapest
Bulgaria
California
Cambodia
Canada East
Canada West / Rockies
& Vancouver
Cape Town &
Garden Route
Cape Verde
Channel Islands
Chicago & The Lakes
China
Cologne
Copenhagen
Corfu
Costa Blanca
& Valencia
Costa Brava
Costa del Sol & Granada
Crete
Cuba
Cyprus (North and
South)
Devon & Cornwall
Dresden
Dubai

Dublin
Dubrovnik &
Dalmatian Coast
Edinburgh
Egypt
Egypt Red Sea Resorts
Finland
Florence
Florida
French Atlantic Coast
French Riviera
(Nice, Cannes & Monaco)
Fuerteventura
Gran Canaria
Greece
Hamburg
Hong Kong & Macau
Iceland
India
India South
Ireland
Israel
Istanbul
Italy
Japan
Jordan
Kos
Krakow
Lake Garda
Lanzarote
Las Vegas
Lisbon
London
Los Angeles
Madeira & Porto Santo
Madrid
Mallorca
Malta & Gozo
Mauritius
Menorca

Milan
Montenegro
Morocco
Munich
Naples & Amalfi Coast
New York
New Zealand
Norway
Oslo
Oxford
Paris
Peru & Bolivia
Phuket
Portugal
Prague
Rhodes
Rome
Salzburg
San Francisco
Santorini
Sardinia
Scotland
Seychelles
Shanghai
Sicily
Singapore
South Africa
Sri Lanka
Stockholm
Switzerland
Tenerife
Thailand
Turkey
Turkey South Coast
Tuscany
United Arab Emirates
USA Southwest
(Las Vegas, Colorado,
New Mexico, Arizona
& Utah)
Venice
Vienna
Vietnam
Zakynthos & Ithaca,
Kefalonia, Lefkas

The travel guides with
Insider
Tips

INDEX

This index lists all places, destinations and beaches featured in this guide. Numbers in bold indicate a main entry.

CREDITS

WRITE TO US

e-mail: info@marcopologuides.co.uk

Did you have a great holiday?
Is there something on your mind?
Whatever it is, let us know!
Whether you want to praise, alert us to errors or give us a personal tip – MARCO POLO would be pleased to hear from you.
We do everything we can to provide the very latest information for your trip.

Nevertheless, despite all of our authors' thorough research, errors can creep in. MARCO POLO does not accept any liability for this. Please contact us by e-mail or post.

MARCO POLO Travel Publishing Ltd Pinewood, Chineham Business Park Crockford Lane, Chineham Basingstoke, Hampshire RG24 8AL United Kingdom

PICTURE CREDITS
Cover Photograph: Cala Llombards (Gettyimages: J. Greuel)
Photos: DuMont Bildarchiv: Schwarzbach (124, 130); f1online (62); f1online/age (18 bottm); Gettyimages: J. Greuel (1); Gettyimages/Westend61 (3); Gettyimages: Calamorlanda (84/85), K. F. Schöfmann (18 centre); R. Hackenberg (75, 131); huber-images: H. P. Huber (48, 53), R. Schmid (5, 32/33, 96/97); laif: T. Gerber (flap right, 58, 98), M. Gonzalez (28 right, 44); Heuer (4 top, 4 bottom, 80, 88, 118), G. Knechtel (28 left), G. Lengler (29), T. Linkel (30/31, 37, 83, 86/87, 104), N. Martensen (38); laif/Le Figaro Magazine: Fautre (114, 133); laif/robertharding: R. Tomlinson (95); laif/Zenit: P. Langrock (72); Look: P. Chichester (54), H. Dressler (43, 60/61), R. Mirau (144/145), T. Roetting (24, 129), Roetting/Pollex (flap left), D. Schoenen (34); Look/age fotostock (6, 19 top, 91, 92, 102); mauritius images: S. Beuthan (15), M. Habel (76/77), M. Lange (78), E. Wrba (111); mauritius images/age (17, 106/107, 122/123); mauritius images/age fotostock: T. Balaguer (7), M. Mayol (18 top), S. Torrens (71); mauritius images/Alamy (8, 9, 11, 126/127, 132 o., 132 bottom); mauritius images/Axiom Photographic: I. Cumming (40/41); mauritius images/Cultura: W. Perugini (2), R. Rohde (19 bottom); mauritius images/imagebroker: T. Haupt (101), K. Kreder (65), M. Moxter (57), STELLA (69); mauritius images/John Warburton-Lee: D. Pearson (23); mauritius images/Westend61: M. Moxter (46/47), A. Sass (26/27); picture-alliance/dpa (121); Schapowalow/4Corners: R. Taylor (66/67); O. Stadler (51); vario images/Westend61 (20/21); E. Wrba (12/13, 30, 31, 68, 130/131)

3rd Edition – fully revised and updated 2018
Worldwide Distribution: Marco Polo Travel Publishing Ltd, Pinewood, Chineham Business Park, Crockford Lane, Basingstoke, Hampshire RG24 8AL, United Kingdom. Email: sales@marcopolouk.com
© MAIRDUMONT GmbH & Co. KG, Ostfildern
Chief editor: Marion Zorn
Author: Petra Rossbach; co-authors: Brigitte Kramer, Tom Gebhardt; editor: Felix Wolf
Programme supervision: Lucas Forst-Gill, Susanne Heimburger, Johanna Jiranek, Nikolai Michaelis, Kristin Wittemann
Picture editors: Gabriele Forst, Anja Schlatterer, Stefanie Wiese
What's hot: wunder media, Munich, Brigitte Kramer and Tom Gebhardt
Cartography road atlas and pull-out map: © MAIRDUMONT, Ostfildern
Design cover, p. 1, cover pull-out map: Karl Anders – Büro für Visual Stories, Hamburg; interior: milchhof:atelier, Berlin; design p. 2/3, Discovery Tours: Susan Chaaban Dipl.-Des. (FH)
Translated from German by Kathleen Becker, Susan Jones, Samantha Riffle, Andrea Scheuer, Jennifer Walcoff Neuheiser
Prepress: writehouse, Cologne; InterMedia, Ratingen
Phrase book in cooperation with Ernst Klett Sprachen GmbH, Stuttgart, Editorial by Pons Wörterbücher

MIX
Paper from responsible sources
FSC® C124385

DOS & DON'TS

There are a few things you should keep in mind during your visit to Mallorca

HIKING UNPREPARED

Don't underestimate the dangers of mountain hikes; they often start at sea level and go up beyond 1,000 m/3,280 ft. Don't head for the mountains without a hiking guide (human or in book form) and make sure you have all the necessary gear (hiking footwear, raingear, sun protection, water, etc.) with you.

RIP-OFF CARRIAGE RIDES

Not every carriage driver has the same definition of "guided tour" as you. Agree on the price before you start out and don't pay more than 40 euros for half an hour.

TOUCH JELLYFISH

If you encounter a lion's mane jellyfish while swimming, clean yourself with salt water (not fresh water!) when back on the beach, and scratch off the remains of any nematocysts with a credit card. Use an ice pack or something against insect bites to ease the pain. It's easier to avoid them when you wear a diving mask or goggles. Pay attention to the signs on the beach: a white flag with a violet jellyfish drawing.

DICING WITH DEATH

The dangers of swimming in the sea when the red flag is flying can't be stressed enough. Every year, lives are lost through carelessness or valiant efforts to save careless people. When there's a strong swell, undertows can become lethally dangerous. Be careful around finca or hotel pools too: over a dozen children drown each year because their parents don't pay attention!

PARK ILLEGALLY

Even though many Spaniards tend to wait in a loading zone with their blinkers on or double park, these practices are not legal. A fine can easily cost 100 euros and the notice will even be sent to your home address if you're driving a rental car. If you have paid for your parking ticket or meter, but the time runs out, you can usually do away with the fine by paying a small fee at one of the ticket machines (read the small print on the fine notice).

BIKINIS ON THE BUS

Most tourist hotspots (including the Playa de Palma) have introduced "conduct" rules. "Bucket drinking" or binge fests on public streets, urinating in public and riding the bus in a bikini are prohibited. Although this "Ballermann Etiquette" is hardly enforced, you should nonetheless pay heed to these rules of conduct.